I came to bear witness to the truth
Jn. 18. 37

What is Truth?

John Martin Sahajananada

Foreword
Fr. M. Amaladoss s.j.

**LUC
EDITIONS**

WHAT IS TRUTH?

ISBN: 979-10-91859-02-8
© John Martin Sahajananda and Luc Editions, 2013

All rights reserved. No part of this book may be reproduced or transmitted in any form or by any means, electronic, mechanical, photocopying, recording, or by any information storage and retrieval system, without the prior permission in writing from the publisher.

The views expressed in the book are those of the contributors and the publisher takes no responsibility for any of the statements.

All the Scripture quotes in this volume are the author's own translations, closely inspired by The New Jerusalem Bible.

Published by Luc Editions
6 rue Abbé Tolmer
14530 Luc sur Mer
France

Contact:
LucEditions@mailoo.org

Book and cover design by Agnès Kauffmann
Printed and bound by LSI in the U.K.

A catalogue record for this book is available from the Bibliothèque Nationale de France.

John Martin Sahajananda will soon be publishing a second book with Luc Editions:

THE NEW ANNUNCIATION
(A Universal Call to be Virgin Mothers)

We will be publishing it both in English and in French please check our website for availability:

www.LucEditions.com

To

Sr. Jean Van Hacht, who sustained me,
K. Jojamma, my beloved eldest sister,
Chantal Dautais, my spiritual co-worker.
All have reached the further shore.

Contents

Acknowledgements XI
Foreword XIII
Introduction XVII

The Truth of Jesus

1. Blessed Are Those Who Are Led By Wisdom   3

2. From Authority to Freedom   9
   The "I say unto you" statements of Jesus

3. The Garden of Eden and the Prodigal Son   29
   An archetype of our spiritual evolution

4. In the Foot Prints of Virgin Mary   49

5. Journey to the Inner Jerusalem   59

6. A Dance of Transformation   69

Truth in Dialogue

7. The Prayer of Christopher   75

8. Guidelines for Inter-religious Dialogue   81

9.	Diversity, Uniqueness and Unity	87
10.	Beyond Theism and Atheism	105
11.	The Eternal Self and its Garland	119
12.	One Way–Many Paths *The inclusive way of Christ*	127
13.	Integral Dynamic Monotheism	145
14.	The Formless and the Forms	161
15.	Bearing Witness to the Truth	167
16.	Truth	203

ENDNOTES 209

Acknowledgements

'What is Truth?' is not a new book but rather a collection of articles written at different times and on different occasions. Hence certain repetitions are inevitable and so I appeal to the patience of the readers.

Four articles, 'Guidelines to Inter-Religious Dialogue', 'Diversity, Uniqueness and Unity', 'Integral Dynamic Monotheism' and 'Beyond Theism and Atheism' were first published on the website of Monastic Inter-religious Dialogue. The Vidhya Jyothi Journal of Theological Reflection, New Delhi, has published two articles: 'The Inclusive Way of Christ' and 'Bearing Witness to the Truth'. I have revised all these articles as some expressions needed to be clarified and qualified. I am very grateful to Br. Gregory Person, the Secretary of Monastic Inter-religious Dialogue, and Fr. Fernand s.j., the Editor of Vidyayoti, New Delhi, for their kind permission to include the above-mentioned articles in this book. I express my heartfelt thanks and gratitude for their support and encouragement.

I am extremely grateful to Fr. M. Amaladoss s.j., for writing the Foreword to this book. His suggestions and corrections were very important for me. I am also very grateful to Michael Highburger for sparing his valuable time to read the manuscript and writing an introduction to it even though he was very busy over Christmas-time. I would like to express my thanks and gratitude to Yvonne Lanners who has read some of the articles and suggested many corrections and additions. Her moral and spiritual support is very much appreciated. I would like to thank Sneha Jyothi (Heike) who has read many of the articles and has given valuable suggestions and corrections. Her encouragement and moral support have been a great source of strength. Finally I would like to thank all my friends in UK, France, Belgium, Spain, Ireland, Germany and Luxemburg who have encouraged me to publish this book. I am very grateful to my brothers in Shantivanam who have always supported my endeavours.

Finally I would like to thank Eric Callcut and Luc Editions, France, who have accepted to publish this book.

11.02.2013

Foreword

God is a mystery beyond name and form. All that we can really say about God is neti, neti; not this-not that.

Apophatic or negative theologies are known in Europe too. St. Thomas Aquinas said: we know that God is; we do not know what God is. But this does not stop people from trying to speak about God. We may not be able to know God. But we can experience God, because God is the deepest basis of our being. We are in God and God is in us. Experience always seeks to express itself. This happens largely through symbols, stories, parables, narrative. Unfortunately traditional Scholastic theology seeks for conceptual clarity and in the process misses a true vision of God. The Scholastic theologians were inspired by Aristotle, who based his metaphysics on his physics or the knowledge of the material world. This world can be known by our senses and by the concepts that our intellect abstracts from them. When we try to project such abstract concepts on to metaphysical realities, they prove quite inadequate. One speaks of analogy. But analogy is nothing but a blind projection. It can hardly bring us true knowledge of what transcends our senses. So the mystics often use evocative symbols to evoke in the hearers, not necessarily knowledge, but experience. Perhaps one can say experiential knowledge.

The Scholastic theologians projected on God their perception of human makers of various objects, like a potter who makes pots. So they saw God as the maker of the world. The world was outside God. Of course, God was said to have created it out of nothing. A world that exists and functions by itself outside God can eventually do so without God, like a watch that can run without a watch maker. This is how Europe gets secularized; holding on to and manipulating the watch, while ignoring the watch-maker. The Indian and Chinese (Taoist) traditions saw the relations between God and the universe in more organic terms. There were tendencies like some Tantric schools which saw the world simply as an emanation of God. The world then is simply unreal and an illusion. But the great thinkers like Shankara and Ramanuja saw the relations between God and the world as non-dual or advaitic. God and the world are neither one nor two, but not-two. Both monism and dualism were denied. While Shankara sees the worldly realities as waves in the ocean, Ramanuja sees the world as the body of God. God and the world are internally related so that they can be called one in being and yet the world is different, though dependent on God, so that they can be considered two: they are not-two. This is a mystery that should not be thought about but experienced. It has always attracted mystics wherever they come from. Swami Abhishiktananda (Henri Le Saux) and Swami Dayananda (Bede Griffiths) were two such mystics who made their home in Shantivanam in South India.

Brother John Martin is a disciple who comes from that spiritual-mystic tradition. The book that you have in your hands is talking about such experiential knowledge. It is a collection of reflections, stories, parables and poems. It is evocative and provocative. At a first reading it might seem unfamiliar to readers schooled in traditional Scholastic theology. But if you stop thinking and start praying you may achieve experience and insight. This is not an academic thesis, but an introduction to experience. It must be read, not conceptually, but with a symbolic imagination rooted in life-experience of the divine.

Our guarantee for such an advaitic vision is Jesus Christ, the God-Man. He not only realizes the advaitic union in himself, but he also shares it with all humans. (cf. Jn 17:21) St. Peter, followed by Sts. Irenaeus and Athanasius, speak of our participation in the divine nature. The Greek Fathers spoke of the process of salvation as divinization. The Latin Church quietly abandoned this tradition. Its legal mind could not match the mystical vision. Scholastic theology too was unable to reach out to such transcendent realities.

I think that it is the task of the Indian church to rediscover and rearticulate such divine visions. This is possible because of our ongoing dialogue with the Hindu tradition. So I heartily welcome Brother John Martin's book. Being a pioneering effort, one or other formulation may seem provocative. But be patient and focus on the experience and the vision. Imagine that in Jesus we too have become gods. You will not have words to easily express this experience. Then you will be more understanding of Brother John Martin's efforts.

Brother Martin sees life as a journey growing into different levels of consciousness leading us to our experience of oneness with God. Jesus too traversed this way as a human being, though he was one with God in being in a way that we are not. Yet Jesus is inviting us to become like him. This growth in consciousness also involves a growth in the way we experience and understand God. Human, religious history may follow a same pattern. Even secularism may play a role in breaking our limited images of God. That is why Pope Benedict XVI invited agnostics to a meeting of religious leaders in Assisi. The many parables and stories in this book turn around the same teaching.

Finally what is important is not that you merely intellectually understand this book, but that you start searching for that experience of becoming divine. May Jesus Christ be your guide and may the Spirit of God be the transforming force.

Michael Amaladoss, s.j
Institute of Dialogue with Cultures and Religions, Chennai, India.
December 8, 2011.

Introduction:
What is Truth?

Pilate said to him, 'So, then you are a king?' Jesus answered, 'It is you who says that I am a king. I was born for this, to bear witness to the truth; and all who are on the side of truth listen to my voice'. Pilate said, 'What is truth?' And so saying he went out again to the Jews and said, 'I find no case against him.'

John 18:37-38

Over the centuries and throughout the ages questions about the nature of truth have plagued great thinkers, not only the eminent philosophers of ancient Greece and Rome but in fact all cultures and peoples. Yet it is not clear what Pilate's intention is here. Does he really want to know what truth is or is he only mocking Jesus? Is his question made in a sarcastic, patronizing tone, dismissing Jesus' words, or even worse, plainly contemptuous? Or could it be something altogether different? Could it be that in a younger, more idealistic phase of his life, Pilate himself had taken up this question in earnest only to abandon it in the face of the frustration, cynicism and weariness that a life void of faith and lasting meaning invariably brings; and so, resigning himself to his scepticism, he chose to deem all such inquiries as futile, finally turning his attention to more practical matters like politics, statecraft and the pursuit of wealth? Or a still more unique reading would be that Pilate's dismissal is actually a feeble attempt at kind-heartedness. Sensing Jesus' sincerity, Pilate is genuinely and sympathetically (though

xviii WHAT IS TRUTH?

perhaps nihilistically) intending to ask, 'Is enigmatic, unattainable truth really worth giving up your life for?' To be sure, Pilate does not know who it is he is speaking to, and so does not feel inclined to wait for Jesus' response. But to his credit he at least goes out to the crowd to speak in Jesus' defense: 'I find no guilt in him.'

For Jesus' part what is it that he has come to bear witness to? Earlier in the same gospel we hear: 'even if I testify on my own behalf, my testimony is valid, for I know where I came from and where I am going. But you have no idea where I come from or where I am going.' (John 8.14) And in the prologue: 'the Word became flesh and made his dwelling among us. We have seen his glory, the glory of the One and only, who came from the Father, full of grace and truth... For the law was given through Moses; grace and truth came through Jesus Christ.' (John 1:14-17) But what is this truth that comes through Jesus Christ? What is *truth*?

Linguists tell us that the English word 'truth' (also 'troth', 'betroth', 'truce', 'trust') derives from the ancient Germanic *treww* (faithful) and ultimately the Indo-European *dru* (wood, tree) which gives rise to the English 'tree'[1] and accesses a semantic field that would include adjectives like 'firm', 'sturdy' 'solid', 'trusty', 'unchanging', 'unmoving', as might be personified by any full-grown European oak. The Sanskrit *Sathya* also signifies 'unchangeable' and has a broad range of related connotations: 'true', 'real', 'actual', 'genuine', 'sincere', 'honest', 'truthful', 'faithful', 'pure', 'virtuous', 'good', 'that which is beyond distinctions of time, space and person', 'that which pervades the universe in all its constancy'. *Sat* has as its root *as,* 'to be' (cognate to English 'is') and is

---

1. John Ayto, *Word Origins: Secret Histories of English Words from A-Z*, (A & C Black Publishers Ltd, 37 Soho Square, London W1D 3QZ, 2nd ed., 2005), p. 519.

probably an antecedent of 'sate' and 'satisfy', i.e. 'to fill', 'to be filled'. Like the English 'truth', *sat* functions in the philosophical sense as 'absolute', 'eternal', 'unchanging Being'. (*Asato ma sat gamaya*–Lead me from the unreal to Real).[2]

In John 14.6 Jesus says 'I am the Way, the truth, and the life.'[3] But the reverse would be equally valid: the Way, the truth and the life is 'I AM'. (Compare John 8:58: 'very truly, I tell you, before Abraham was, I AM'). In either case, Jesus is that which he comes to bear witness to. Jesus the *man* bears witness to the *Christ* which IS his most essential Being. Signifier and signified merge into a perfect whole like the proverb about the sandalwood tree: *each part is It*. Even the tiniest sliver of the sandalwood tree carries the glorious scent of sandal. And so John 14.6 which has so often been enlisted in the service of sectarian polemics as proof of Christianity's privileged place in the pantheon of world religions, actually bears witness to a universality that transcends all religions, dogmas, creeds and sectarian boundaries. I AM knows no name, form, time, place, culture or people but is the source and fundamental endowment of all humanity.

The following collection of articles attempts to shed light on Pilate's question and on the paradoxical nature of the person of Jesus–the one who bears witness to something is the one who points back to himself, beyond form and particularity, to the eternal which is his very own Self. It attempts to shed light on the paradoxical nature of Reality, which at root is a non-dual Reality–a single, undivided unity on the one hand and the entirety of the multiplicity of all phenomena and form on the other; it is the Mystery which cannot be directly apprehended by the

---

2. See also Chapter 15.
3. See Chapter 12 for an extended discussion.

mind and the senses, cannot be reduced to any formal system no matter how elegant, and yet is available to any sincere aspirant through the discipline of faith.

These essays, which draw on Biblical exegesis, Hindu *sastra* and the wisdom traditions of various cultures and religions, suggest diverse aspects of (Christian) religious life and function in a dialogical way to uncover alternate modes of understanding the person of Christ and the spiritual quest. The attempt is neither discursive nor analytical, much less is it intended as a comprehensive hermeneutic but rather is a polyphonic sounding which as a whole combines to fill in gaps where no single voice on its own could be relied upon, while, as a collectivity, endeavours to point to the ineffable in fuller measure.

Chapter 2 explores the *Sermon on the Mount* and presents Jesus, the embodiment of the New Covenant, as the one who frees us from the earlier dispensation. Chapter 3 looks at the Prodigal Son story and, among other things, deciphers the classical motif of departure (like the exile from the Garden of Eden) where the hero's leave-taking brings him to the test to suffer loneliness and vulnerability–but transformation and renewal as well, ('from unconscious unity to conscious unity')–and return, where he is able to serve in a new way by virtue of the humility and wisdom gained on the way. Chapter 4 utilizes the image of Mary in re-envisioning a new Church. Chapter 5 is the journey home, the walk with Christ that leads back to Jerusalem while the short essay in Chapter 6 employs the metaphor of the dance to celebrate this walk. Chapters 7, 11 and 14 are allegories of young seekers who find true teachers to guide them in the way. Chapter 8 looks at truth in the interreligious context and extols dialogue at the level of 'eternal truth', rather than that of 'historical truth'. Chapter 9, in comparing Hinduism, Buddhism and Christianity, whose starting points are quite different, shows that the source of the three is actually identical. Chapter 10 looks at another type of dialogue, the conversation between theists and atheists. The atheist's bid for autonomy is seen to have a healthy dimension insofar as it is a rebellion against autocratic theological structures and naïve images of God. But the atheist suffers dislocation and alienation having, so to speak, *thrown the baby out with the bathwater*, finding himself devoid of any principle of transcendence. Chapter 12 takes up the verse, 'I am the way, the truth and the life', and conjectures that there is indeed only one way, that of giving up the narcissistic centre–the ego; there is only one way, the way of God. However Jesus' message in this verse is not intended to be 'exclusive' but universal and all-inclusive, transcending religious, ethnic and cultural boundaries. Chapter 13 distinguishes wisdom traditions (e.g. Buddhism and Hinduism) from prophetic traditions (e.g. Judaism, Christianity, and Islam) and further identifies various forms of Hindu monotheism: *advaita*, qualified non-duality, duality, etc., and compares them with Jesus' teaching. The final chapter, 'Bearing Witness to the Truth' covers a broad range of issues, from revelation to Biblical and Vedic traditions, from non-dual wisdom to *sathyam,* and serves to synthesize questions raised in earlier essays, compressing and directing the discussion to and through the prism of Jesus who is simultaneously 'the fullness of truth and the fullness of revelation' where non-dualistic wisdom and non-dualistic action 'come together in love'.

Michael Highburger
Shantivanam, Advent 2011

The Truth of Jesus

I.
Blessed are those who are led by Wisdom

Blessed are those who place themselves
Under the wings of wisdom,
She protects them as a mother protects her child,
She nourishes them with the milk from her breast.

She is all penetrating and elusive.
It is not possible to touch her.
It is not possible to see her,
It is not possible to accumulate her.

She is as light as a feather.
Those who have her can fly like birds,
And they can walk on the waters of desire,
Without being drowned.

4 What is Truth?

Wisdom is as simple as milk,
As eternal as wine
And as sweet as honey.
Those who follow her

Live in the land flowing with milk and honey,
And their cup is always filled with the wine of immortality.

Wisdom gives herself to those who trust her,
She gives only when it is necessary,
As a mother feeds her child.

We cannot accumulate her by force,
When one tries to acquire her she will disappear.
When one tires to accumulate her she will become useless
As manna in the desert.
Wisdom cannot be written down
The moment one writes it down
It turns into knowledge.

Wisdom is as eternal as God,
She was there when God unfolded the world,
But she is as new as a new-born babe.

Those who are guided by wisdom are like those
Who are guided by a child.
The child cannot walk but leads them,
The child cannot see but shows the way,
The child does not know but teaches.

Wisdom is not a quantity but quality,
But she fills all things.
She is as gentle as a mother to her child,
She does not place burdens on the shoulders.
Those who follow her are without burdens.

Wisdom reveals the eternal nature of human beings,
Only she knows the immortal nature,
Because she herself is immortal.

We cannot control the wisdom
But she controls everything.
We cannot predict her
But she knows all.
Mysterious is the nature of wisdom.

She is always vigilant
And protects her children
As a hen protects her little ones.
To those who place themselves under her care,
She penetrates into their hearts and reveals
The profound egoistic desires hidden in their hearts.

She is all penetrating
And nobody can hide anything from her eyes.
She is as bright as the Sun,
And as powerful as the rays of the Sun.
Her presence melts the desires
Which have become like ice
On which people have built their houses.

She is as compassionate as a mother to her invalid child,
But at the same time as ruthless as death,
She does not preserve anything that is not real.

We cannot search for wisdom.
She herself comes to those,
Who are humble and pure of heart.
Blessed are those who have found her favour.

She comes as rain to a dry land,

She comes as a child to a sterile woman,

She comes as sight to the blind,

She comes as life to the dead,

She comes as riches to the poor,

She comes as light to those who are in darkness.

Blessed are those who have found her favour.

She is more precious than all the things of the world,

There is nothing in the world equal to her.

Those who have found her favour can be free from the Power of the world,

That is the Desire to acquire and to become.

2.
From authority to freedom

The 'I say unto you' statements of Jesus

The 'I say unto you' statements of Jesus are a part of the Sermon on the Mount in Mathew's gospel and the Sermon on the Plain in the gospel of Luke. In the gospel of Mathew they are much more elaborative than in the gospel of Luke. So I will focus on the gospel of Mathew. In general people think that Jesus, in these statements, is proposing a new law or a new standard of how to live to his followers. But this way of interpreting his teaching does not do justice to Jesus Christ, to his message and to his mission. The 'I say unto you' statements of Jesus' have to be understood in the context of the new covenant that God promised through the prophets. The 'I say unto you' statements are an invitation to grow from the Law written on the Tablets of Stone to the Law written in the heart; from the God of authority to the God of freedom, from the God of words to the God of silence, from God outside to God within.

The Prophet Jeremiah says 'Look the days are coming, Yahweh declares, when I shall make a new covenant with the house of Israel (and the House of Judah) but not like the covenant I made with their ancestors the day I took them out of Egypt, a covenant which they broke, even though I was their Master, Yahweh declares. No this is the covenant I shall make with the House of Israel when those days have come, Yahweh declares. Within them I shall plant my Law, writing it on their hearts. Then I shall be their God and they will be my people.

There will be no further need for everyone to teach neighbour or brother, saying, 'learn to know Yahweh!' No, they will all know me, from the least to the greatest, Yahweh declares. Since I shall forgive their guilt and never more call their sin to mind'.[1]

In the first covenant, God gave the Ten Commandments to the Jewish people through Moses. In them he told them what they should do and what they should not do. But this arrangement never worked properly. People, many times, broke the laws of God. Scripture says that they were always unfaithful to God. So God promised the New Covenant in which he will write the law in the hearts of the people and they will follow the law of God spontaneously, without being told. There is no need one person telling another to know God but from the least to the greatest everyone knows God. In fact God does not write this law in the hearts newly, as he has already written it when he created human beings. Yet most human beings are not conscious of it. To write the law in their hearts only means to make people remember who they really are. It is to make them realize their original self. It is also discovering our original image and likeness of God. It is re-entering into the Garden of Eden.

Four moments in the life of Jesus, before his death and resurrection, seem to be in a special way important. The first moment was his birth as a human being, through Mary, his physical mother. The second moment was the day of his circumcision in which he became a Jew. As a Jew he lived the Ten Commandments given by God. The third moment was his baptismal experience in which he came out of the womb of Judaism and entered into the direct experience of God. The fourth moment was when he realized that he and God (the Father) were one. The first moment was the birth of his individual consciousness, the second was the birth of his collective consciousness, the third moment was the birth of his universal consciousness (the Son of God) and the fourth was the birth of his unitary consciousness.

Let us take the symbol of a tree. A tree has leaves, branches, a trunk and roots. The leaves represent our individual identities. The branches represent our collective identities, the trunk represents our universal consciousness and the roots represent our unitary consciousness. Jesus began as a leaf, connected himself to the Jewish branch at the time of his circumcision, entered into the trunk at the moment of his baptism and then finally realized his unity with the Father, the roots. Now he is the whole tree. He embraces within himself all these levels.

When Jesus had his experience of God at his baptism the heavens were opened and the spirit of God came upon him and he heard the voice of God 'You are my beloved Son, with whom I am well pleased'.[2] God did not reveal to him any commandments, even not the so called two great commandments: The Love of God and the Love of neighbour. God only told him 'you are my beloved Son'. God revealed who Jesus was. That is the essence of the new covenant. This self-knowledge becomes the way, the truth and the life. There are no more external laws or commandments.

A person who lives according to the first covenant says that the Law is the way, the truth and the life. A person who lives according to the New Covenant says: 'I am the way, the truth and the life.' This experience of Jesus was a fulfilment and a revolution. It was a fulfilment because it was the inauguration of the new covenant promised by God through the prophets. It was a revolution because it was the birth of a human being or human consciousness that was greater than religion. A pregnant woman finds fulfilment when she gives birth to a child. So also a religion finds fulfilment when she gives birth to a human being who is greater than she is. We can say that at the moment of Jesus' baptism his religion became a mother, until then she was only a pregnant woman. This experience of Jesus also was a transition from the God of authority to the God of freedom. It is a transition from the collective consciousness into the universal consciousness. In the collective consciousness (the first or Old Testament), God speaks often and with authority, with rewards and punishments–but in the universal consciousness (the second or New Covenant) God speaks only twice and he says the same thing each time: 'you are my beloved son' or 'he is my beloved son'.[3]

The primary mission of Jesus was to inaugurate the New Covenant, a new human consciousness, to invite human beings to the experience of the New Covenant. Jesus does it by proclaiming the good news of the kingdom of God: 'The time is fulfilled, the kingdom of God is at hand, repent and believe in the good news'.[4] Mathew has a short version: 'Repent, for the kingdom of heaven is at hand'. This kingdom of God is the experience of the New Covenant in which God writes the law in the hearts of the people. It is also the inauguration of a new human being who can say 'I am the way, the truth and the life'.

We have to understand the general teachings of Jesus and his 'I say unto you' statements, from the ideal of the New Covenant or universal consciousness.

I SAY UNTO YOU

The 'I say unto you' statements are made by the universal consciousness or by the person who had the experience of the New Covenant. The universal consciousness never makes laws for others. A person who lives in the universal consciousness says 'I am the way, the truth and the life' and invites others to grow into the same consciousness. This person is free from the past and the future. He is free from the past because he has transcended the collective mind of the past. He is free from the future because he does not become the collective mind to the future. He gives freedom to the future. The present is for the sake of the present and the future is for the sake of the future. This is the greatness and the humility of the statement: I am the way, the truth and the life.

So when we read the 'I say unto you' statements of Jesus, we should not look at them as a new standard of living. They are just an invitation to grow into the universal consciousness or into the new covenant. Jesus was not replacing the old collective consciousness (the Torah) with his new collective consciousness. He was not telling people what they should do and should not do. If he had done so then he would have been introducing a new collective consciousness and thus in fact closing the door to the new covenant. It would have been against his mission because any collective consciousness becomes exclusive. The question we need to ask is how a person who is living in the new covenant or universal consciousness reacts to the collective consciousness of his tradition, in the case of Jesus, the Torah.

Jesus takes six issues of the Torah: thou shall not kill; thou shall not commit adultery; not divorce with the writ of dismissal; you must not break your oath but must fulfil your oaths to the Lord; eye for an eye and tooth for a tooth; you will love your neighbour and hate your enemies.[5]

Thou shall not kill

'You have heard how it was said to our ancestors, you shall not kill and if anyone does kill he must answer for it before the court.

> *But I say this to you: Anyone who is angry... anyone who calls his brother 'Fool'... anyone who calls him 'Traitor' will answer for it in hellfire.'*

According to the first covenant or old covenant, the external Law guides human beings. This law is not something they have discovered in their search but have been told by someone else as an authority. In this case it was God. There is an inherent tendency in human beings to kill so, in order to control that tendency, the law says: do not kill. Here human beings live in individual consciousness, individual desires and ambitions dominate. These desires have to be controlled for the sake of social good so the common law is established. In individual consciousness and collective consciousness there are others, who are seen as essentially different from one another.

But to a person who lives in the universal consciousness, others, in an essential sense, do not exist, though they exist functionally. In this consciousness, to kill others is to kill oneself, to get angry with others is to get angry with oneself, to call some one a 'fool' is to call oneself a 'fool', to call someone a 'traitor' is to call oneself a 'traitor'. In the Isa Upanishad of Indian scriptures it says: a sage is one who has become all. He does not hurt himself by hurting others. To hurt others is to hurt him or herself. For a sage, others do not exist. Whatever he or she does, he or she does to himself or herself. This is also the essence of the new covenant, the kingdom of God. Jesus said: 'Whatever you do to the least of my brothers and sisters that you do unto me'. But one has to grow into it. It cannot be practiced as a law or as a standard. If it is so then it becomes a burden. So when Jesus said: do not get angry with your brother, do not call your brother a 'fool' and do not call your brother a 'traitor'; we should not take it as a law or standard. We have to go to the source from which we discover that all of these things are sins against ourselves, because we are all one and there are no others.

Functionally there may be a necessity to get angry and to call some one a name. Jesus was angry with the Scribes and Pharisees. He called them 'hypocrites'. He called Herod a 'fox'. He was angry in the temple and chased people away. He called Peter 'Satan'. But they belong to his functional level. There is anger that comes from our individual identification, which may lead to individual killing. There is also anger that comes from our collective identification, which may lead to collective killings. All wars belong to the collective level. There is anger that comes from our universal identification. But this anger does not kill anyone. It comes from love. This anger belongs to the functional level. So we need to distinguish between the anger that belongs to the functional level and the anger that belongs to the essential level. Parents may get angry with their children because they wish for their well-being and growth. It comes out of love. If we take the words of Jesus literally and try to follow them, it may happen that we create psychological problems for ourselves. Suppressing or repressing anger because of an ideal can create inner violence. It may block the psychological growth of a person. But when we discover our universal consciousness then we have the freedom to get angry or not to get angry, to call someone with a name or not. The new covenant is not an ideal, it is freedom from all ideals. Jesus is inviting people to grow into freedom and act from there.

You must not commit adultery

> *'You have heard how it was said, you must not commit adultery. But I say this to you, if a man looks at a woman lustfully; he has already committed adultery with her in his heart'.*

In the first covenant, people live in a dualistic relationship with God and with one another. Adultery is when a married person enters into sexual relationship with another person outside marriage. It is a kind of inner violence, not respecting the dignity of one's spouse. Where there is betrayal there is inner violence. So adultery is forbidden by the Law. But a man or a woman who lives in the new covenant or universal consciousness realizes that the other one is the unique manifestation of God just as he or she is also a unique manifestation of God. There is nothing wrong in looking at a woman or a man. We need to look at each other. But the problem is looking at a man or a woman lustfully. To look at a woman lustfully or to look at a man lustfully is to reduce her or him to a sexual object. We want to possess the other one as an object. It is to take away his or her dignity. When do we take away his or her dignity? It is only when we forget our own dignity as the image and likeness of God. Lustful looking comes from forgetting our human dignity and adultery comes from that forgetfulness.

But again we cannot take the words of Jesus literally and raise it as a standard and impose it on our consciousness. We need to purify our consciousness until we become aware of this truth. This should come out of understanding not as a law to be imposed. There are so many reasons why we become lustful. When we are not aware of our human dignity as the image and likeness of God, we feel that we are empty and from this emptiness come desires. When we do not receive sufficient love and affection as children, that creates an emotional emptiness in us. That emptiness also manifests as lust. There are three archetypal desires; desire for lust, desire of wealth and desire for power. Lust is a kind of greediness for affection, desire for wealth is kind of greediness for material security, and desire for power is a kind of greediness for domination. We try to fill our emptiness from these three desires. Ultimately these desires also are desires for love, for God–but perverted, moving in the wrong direction. The traditional three vows of poverty, obedience and chastity in religious life are meant to curtail these tendencies in the human consciousness. But we cannot curtail them just by making vows. They may take different forms. They may even get perverted.

There are different ways of looking at the opposite sex: to look from our emptiness, from our lust and greed or to look from our dignity of image and likeness of God. If we look from our image and likeness of God then the other also is the image and likeness of God. If we see from our lust or emptiness then the other becomes our object. Sin is acting against our own human dignity. But unfortunately we cannot begin where Jesus has arrived. We cannot see with the eyes of Jesus. We can only see with our conditioned eyes. We have to begin where we are and purify our consciousness slowly and arrive at the ideal that Jesus has realized.

Tear out your right eye—cut off your right hand

'If your right eye should be your downfall, tear it out and throw it away; for it will do you less harm to lose one part of yourself than to have your whole body thrown into hell. And if your right hand should be your downfall, cut it off and throw away; for it will do less harm to lose one part of yourself than to have your whole body go to hell.'

Of course we are not expected to follow this literally. If we do that then I do not think there will be anybody in the world with whole body: we all have lustful thoughts coming from our mind and heart. Again the problem is not with the physical eye or the physical hand. We cannot take away our lust by cutting our physical organs. The physical eye cannot commit sin and the physical hand cannot commit sin. It is the inner eye and the inner hand that commit sin. The external organs are the expression of our inner organs out of which they function. It is our inner attitude which sees through our external eye and acts from our external hand. We need to purify our inner eye and inner hand and then we can see without lust and act without lust.

Do not divorce

> 'It has been also said, anyone who divorces his wife must give her a writ of dismissal. But I say this to you, everyone who divorces his wife, except for the case of an illicit marriage, makes her an adulteress; and anyone who marries a divorced woman commits adultery.'

According to Deuteronomy a man can divorce his wife, if she does not please him, with a writ of divorce. Jewish society, at that time, was a patriarchal, male-dominated society. Woman and children had no rights. They were not counted. They were like objects which a man can possess. They could not give witness. But how does a person who lives in the universal consciousness or the new covenant look at this situation? He cannot accept this inequality. He or she cannot accept men treating women like things and divorcing them at will. It is taking away their dignity. Jesus was fighting for the dignity and the equal rights of women. A person who lives in the universal consciousness sees that every human being—male and female—is created in the image and likeness of God. They are equal in the sight of God. Man cannot reduce women into things. In this sense divorce is a sin. It is a sin not because of divorce but because we have reduced the other into an object, less than ourselves. We can sin not only in divorce but also in other ways where we do not see others as equals. We do not give others equal opportunities. A person who lives in the universal consciousness cannot think of divorce. If he or she still does, it is for the growth of the other, particularly for spiritual growth. He or she sees divorce as sin, as against human dignity, because to divorce the other is to divorce one's own self. But again this cannot be taken as a standard. People have to grow into it. There can be many reasons why people want to divorce. Sometimes there can be many genuine reasons. One has to give some exceptions, certain flexibility. People are in different temperaments and psychological dispositions. It may be difficult to live with a person. God will not force such type of relationships. One should not go to two extremes: either completely rejecting any divorce or allowing every divorce. There may be people who want to divorce just because of lust. It is sin. It is against human dignity. Marriage has a deeper purpose in life. It is meant to manifest divine attributes in relationship.

Man and woman constitute two aspects of the divine. Their coming together is coming together of these two aspects of the divine. They become one. God becomes whole in them. Man and woman together constitute the image and likeness of God. Marriage should not be just for physical and emotional purposes. It is meant to help us to realize our unity with the divine. A man manifests one aspects of the divine and a woman manifests another aspect of the divine. A marriage should help to realize these aspects and discover their essential unity with God. Marriage is not just for the procreation and education of children, even though by bringing forth children we participate in the creative process of God. Marriage has higher goals and purposes. Externally there may be divorces but internally no divorce is possible because we are all united in our deepest level with one another and with God. Universal consciousness or the new covenant is the experience of this essential unity. No physical divorce can separate us from that unity. As St. Paul says: 'Who can separate us from the love of God in Christ?' Nobody can. In the same way, what can separate us form our essential unity? No divorce can do that. Again it is not the intention of Jesus to lay down standards but to invite people to grow into this universal consciousness from which people see that divorce is a sin. It is against human dignity. We have to realize also that marriage is a social institution and belongs to the collective consciousness. It is not a divine institution but a human institution—a social need—which has divine approval. All institutions, including the institution of marriage, belong to the evolutionary process of human consciousness. They are human needs and God approves them. But they are not absolute; they do not remain static but evolve. All institutions, including Sabbath and marriage, are meant to be at the service of human beings and not human beings at the service of institutions. A person who moves into the universal consciousness goes beyond marriage and divorce. They, who live in the universal consciousness, need neither an external ceremony of marriage nor divorce. Because in the universal consciousness there is an essential unity and so no marriage is necessary and no divorce is possible. If there is an external ceremony it is for the social need. If there is an external divorce it is for the social need.

Do not break your oath

> *Again you have heard how it was said to your ancestors; you must not break your oath but must fulfil your oaths to the Lord. But I say unto you, do not swear at all… all you need to say is 'Yes' if you mean yes, 'No' if you mean No; anything more than this comes from the Evil One.'*

When we live in the individual consciousness or collective consciousness, we live in time and space. We live in the consciousness of becoming. We have individual desires and collective desires. We have the past, present and future. Making oaths belongs to the individual or collective consciousness. It belongs to the realm of time and space.

We have a dualistic relationship with God and God acts as our benefactor and protector and we make oaths to him. But in the universal consciousness there is no individual movement or collective movement. There our human consciousness becomes the vehicle for the divine consciousness. Jesus said: 'the works which I do are not my own but the Father who dwells in me does his work'. In this type of life a person has no need of making oaths. Oaths have value only when we live for ourselves alone and use God to fulfil our desires. Making oaths belongs to the realm of individual consciousness and the collective consciousness. We can make individual oaths and collective oaths. But when we are at the service of God, it is God's responsibility to take care of our needs. Jesus said: 'first of all, seek you the kingdom of God and its righteousness and all things will be given to you'. A person who lives at the service of God lives in eternity and for eternity. He or she lives for all. He or she does not need to make any oaths. But this is the way of life into which one has to grow. One cannot begin with it.

We cannot begin with the standard that Jesus attained and proposed. We have to begin where we are and grow into it. So as long we live either in the individual consciousness or in the collective consciousness we can continue making oaths and vows, if we think they help us to grow in our relationship with God. There is nothing wrong in it. Jesus did not come to abolish the Law but to fulfil it. But we should not remain at that level only. We need to fulfil it. It is possible only when we grow in the new covenant or universal consciousness where there is no place for making oaths and vows but only the place to say 'yes' to 'yes' and 'no' to 'no'. It is living in the eternal present.

So we should not think that Jesus is laying a new standard to start with. He was inviting people to grow into the kingdom of God which is the New Covenant or universal consciousness and live from there.

Eye for an eye and tooth for a tooth

> 'You have heard how it was said: Eye for an eye and a tooth for tooth. But I say this to you, offer no resistance to the wicked. On the contrary, if anyone hits you on the right cheek, offer him the other as well; if someone wishes to go to the law with you to get your tunic, let him have your cloak as well. And if anyone requires you to go one mile, go two miles with him. Give to anyone who asks you, and if anyone wants to borrow, do not turn away.'

There are two ways of living our life. One is the way of justice and the other is the way of unconditional love. Eye for an eye and tooth for a tooth is a way of justice. The book of Deuteronomy allows that if anyone strikes one eye of a second, the other has the right to compensate it. If anyone knocks out one tooth of another, the person has the right to compensate it. This is the way of justice. A person who lives in the individual consciousness or collective consciousness lives according to the way of justice. But a person who lives in the universal consciousness goes beyond justice. He acts from unconditional love. We should not take literally what Jesus has said and erect that as a standard to live by. Jesus is not proposing a new collective ideal. He is inviting people to go beyond the way of justice, which belongs to either individual or collective consciousness, and act from the way of unconditional love, which belongs to the universal consciousness. In the individual identity and the collective identity one lives either in an individual boundary or in a collective boundary. One needs to defend one's boundary. If one tries to expand one's boundary the result would be war. Jesus did not live in a boundary. He said: 'the foxes have their holes, the birds have their nests but the son of man has nowhere to lie down and rest'. He had no boundaries to defend and no ambition to expand. He embraces everyone already. He invited people to go beyond boundaries. A man came and asked Jesus to advise his brother to divide his father's property between them; Jesus refused to involve himself. It does not mean that one should not have personal belongings but they have functional value and not essential value. In the way of justice one has rights, obligations and duties. But in the way of unconditional love one goes beyond them. In it there are no obligations and duties, only acting from inner freedom. This unconditional love is not a fixed ideal. In it a person knows what to do in a particular situation. No one can lay down a law. Unconditional love gives inner freedom out of which a person acts what is best in a particular situation. If one takes literally what Jesus is saying to do and wants to carry it out as a rule then one will sink into a difficult and burdensome situation. A fixed ideal is mechanical and may become a burden if it is made absolute. Truth is dynamic and creative. It makes a person free. Jesus came to take away all burdens. 'Truth will make you free,' he said.

A person who lives in the universal consciousness does not possess anything as his own or her own. He or she holds everything as a trustee. He or she is aware that everyone has a part in what he possesses. He or she shares with others what he or she has. He or she does not live according to justice but according to unconditional love. He or she does not claim even if he or she is defrauded. One does more than what is required or expected by the Law, not as a duty or obligation but out of freedom. But again one cannot take this as a standard and try to imitate it. One has to grow into it. Jesus was inviting people to go beyond the way of acting from justice and discover God's unconditional love and live from it. It is the Spirit of God that gives freedom to the person to act in a creative way in a given situation. There are no pre-established standards or models even the ones told by Jesus.

Love your neighbour—hate your enemy

> 'You have heard how it was said: You will love your neighbour and hate your enemy. But I say this to you, love your enemies and pray for those who persecute you, so that you may be children of your Father in heaven for he causes his sun to rise on the bad as well as the good, and sends down rain to fall on the upright and the wicked alike. For if you love those who love you, what reward do you get? Do not even the tax collectors do as much? And if you save your greetings for your brothers, are you doing anything exceptional? Do not even the gentiles do as much?'

When we live in individual consciousness we have individual friends and enemies. If we live in collective consciousness we have collective friends and enemies but when we live in the universal consciousness there are only friends but no enemies. If we take the analogy of the tree: at the level of the leaves there can be individual friends and enemies, at the level of the branches there can be collective friends and enemies but at the level of the trunk there can only be friends and no enemies as there is only one trunk.

In Jesus' day there was big discussion about 'who is my neighbour?' When Jesus told them 'to love your neighbour as yourself,' they asked him, 'Who is my neighbour'? They thought their neighbour was only a fellow Jew. Jesus told them the parable of the Good Samaritan. For him a neighbour is everyone who is in need. For Jesus there were no enemies. He loved all and he was all. He loved everyone as himself, as he lived in the universal consciousness. He also loved God as himself. He saw God's unconditional love for everyone in that God causes his sun to rise on everyone both good and bad and in that he sends rain to fall on both righteous and the unrighteous. Jesus had functional friends and functional enemies. Functional friends were those who accepted his teaching and functional enemies were those who did not agree with his teaching. But he had no essential enemies, as everyone was his friend.

When Jesus said 'love your enemies and pray for those who persecute you', we may have the impression that there are enemies to love. But there are no essential enemies. To have essential enemies is to live either in the individual consciousness or in the collective consciousness, at the level of the leaves or at the level of the branches. But to those who live in the universal consciousness, in the trunk, there are no essential enemies though they might have functional enemies amongst those who refuse to grow into universal consciousness.

Jesus prayed to his Father: 'Father, forgive them for they do not know what they are doing'. Jesus felt that they were acting out of ignorance. He cannot ask God to punish them as God loves them too. So to love our enemies is not in an essential sense but only functional as there are no real enemies. Praying for our functional enemies makes our heart expand and reflect the unconditional love of God.

Jesus said: 'you must therefore be perfect, just as your heavenly Father is perfect.' Personally I do not like the word 'perfect' as it implies a process of becoming. God is not perfect. God is Holy, Whole, Eternal and Fullness. God's perfection does not come out of a process of time. Since we are created in the image and likeness of God, we are also holy, whole, eternal and fullness. The purpose of our spiritual journey is not to become perfect but to discover our image and likeness of God, which already exists. So I prefer to say: 'therefore discover your fullness as your heavenly Father is Fullness'. In the individual consciousness and the collective consciousness we have the movement of becoming perfect. In the universal consciousness we discover our original fullness. It is re-entering the Garden of Eden. Jesus described the experience of this discovery through a parable: the kingdom of God is like a man who found a treasure in the field. He went home, sold everything and bought that field. When we discover our fullness we joyfully give up the movement of becoming.

Jesus invited his spiritual tradition to grow in divine-human relationship. He invited it to grow from the collective consciousness into universal consciousness, from the objective law into the inner law, from the first covenant into the new covenant promised by God. Jewish Scriptures had given this possibility but the spiritual leaders neither utilized it nor allowed others to do so. Jesus said to these leaders: 'you have the keys of the kingdom of heaven, neither you enter nor allow others to enter'. Jesus utilized these keys and entered the kingdom of heaven. Thus he opened this possibility to everyone and invited everyone to do so. But his religious authorities did not respond positively. They considered him a blasphemer and ultimately he had to undergo death on the cross.

The primary mission of Jesus was to inaugurate a new human being who can say like him: 'I am the way, the truth and the life.' But this is not something one can begin with, one has to grow into it. It is a growth from the collective consciousness into the universal consciousness, from the God of Authority to the God of Freedom. This process is not a collective journey but individual. Each individual has to make this journey in his or in her own time and phase. It is a narrow path. Jesus said: 'enter by the narrow gate'. Just as a baby comes out of the physical womb, so also each individual has to come out of the collective womb of religion, as Jesus himself did at the moment of his baptism.

Jesus' secondary mission was to transform his religion (in some sense, all religions) into being a nest where this birth can be facilitated. Since his religious authorities did not cooperate with his plan he formed a nucleus of disciples to facilitate this birth. This nucleus is like a nest from which the birth of this new human consciousness can be facilitated. He gives the keys of the kingdom of heaven to this nucleus so that it can utilize these keys to enter the kingdom and facilitate others to do so. There are two types of keys: ordinary keys and the key of the kingdom of heaven. With the ordinary keys we can open the doors and close them. They are the keys of power and authority. But with the keys of the kingdom of heaven we can only open the door but cannot close it. It is like opening the gate of a cage and allowing the birds to fly into freedom. They are the keys of wisdom, which show the limitations of the collective consciousness and open the door to the universal consciousness and from there to the unitary consciousness. They are the keys of humility and service. Jesus washed the feet of his disciples to show them what his mission was and what their mission should be: to make people free.

The 'I say unto you' statements of Jesus are the declarations of a person who has discovered the inner Law, inner truth and inner freedom. They are the affirmations of the dignity of human beings, manifested in the image and likeness of God, who are greater than the external fixed laws. They are the statements of a person who has replaced the heart of stone with the heart of flesh, the first (old) covenant with the New Covenant, the God of authority with the God of freedom. These statements are not meant to be followed or imitated; they are an invitation to grow into freedom and to declare as Jesus does: 'I am the way, the truth and the life'.

Jesus said: 'I am the light of the world' and 'you are the light of the world'. This is the essence of the new covenant and the good news of Jesus. 'There will be no further need for everyone to teach neighbour or brother saying, learn to know Yahweh! No, they all will know me form the least to the greatest, declares Yahweh.'[6]

3.
THE GARDEN OF EDEN AND THE PRODIGAL SON

An Archetype of Our Spiritual Evolution

Jesus Christ proclaimed the kingdom of God and invited his listeners to grow into this kingdom. It is growing into the radical love of God and the radical love of neighbour. It is our unity with God and with one another. To realize this unity we need to grow in our relationship with God. Our spiritual life is a journey, it is an evolution. It can be described as a journey from unconscious unity to conscious unity. Jesus described this journey in two parables: the parable of the mustard seed and the parable of the Prodigal Son. Jesus said, 'The kingdom of God is like a mustard seed. It is the smallest of all seeds but when it grows, it becomes so big that the birds of the air will come and make their nests in it'.[7] The seed is the symbol of unconscious unity and the tree is the symbol of conscious unity. The tree is in the seed but it is unconscious. What is unconscious has to become conscious. We all come from God and we all return to God. We are all one with God from the beginning of our life but we are not conscious of it. We need to become conscious of it. The parable of the Prodigal son reveals the same truth. This will be explained in detail later. When spiritual persons realize their unity with God they also realize that that unity had been their original state. It is like coming back to one's own home. There are seven levels of mind or consciousness that human beings go through in their evolutionary process to become conscious of their original unity with God.

The first level can be described as unconscious unity. It is our unity with God before we are created or manifested or separated from God. It is better not to speak much about it now. We will know about it at the end.

The second level of mind can be described as unconscious mutual indwelling or unconscious universal mind. It is like the mind of a fœtus in the womb of a woman. A fœtus lives by the life of a woman. There is no real separation between fœtus and woman. They are not two and at the same time not one as there is a new life in the womb. This stage can extend even to the stage after the child is born. After the birth there is a physical separation yet they are bound emotionally. The newborn child has an unconditioned mind. It has no name, no religion, no culture, and no language. Mother and child are intimately connected. Children are naked but they are not ashamed. They do not know good and evil.

The third level of mind can be described as the social mind or the conditioned mind. As a child grows society conditions it with a name, a religion, a language and a culture. The child is taught what is good and what is bad. What it should do and what it should not do. In this mind society is more important than an individual. An individual has to conform to society. If an individual does not conform to the social mind he or she will be excommunicated or outlawed or considered anti-social.

The fourth level of mind can be called 'rebellious individual mind'. It is the stage when an individual starts emerging and would like to affirm its individuality. Individuals start rebelling against the social mind represented by parents, teachers and priests. Religions, as belief structures, also belong to the social mind. In this stage an individual may do things which society considers immoral or dangerous to society. In this sense an individual may become destructive to himself and to the society. In this level an individual is more important than society. Everything revolves around the individual.

The fifth level of mind can be called mature individual mind or consciousness. In this mind an individual uses his or her reason and understands things for himself or herself. In the mature individual mind reason finds a very important role. The period of enlightenment can be called the period of mature mind. In this a person realizes that he or she is not an isolated individual but part and parcel of society and he or she cannot do what he or she likes to do. An individual feels responsible to society and realizes his or her interconnectedness to the whole of humanity and creation. This responsibility becomes too much for an individual to handle. This condition brings a person to surrender himself or herself to the divine. In this surrender God takes the responsibility of the person concerned and the individual feels free and light. In this surrender a person enters into the universal mind or merges with the universal mind. In other words the individual mind grows into the universal mind. This universal mind is the sixth level of consciousness. In this universal mind a person says 'I am in God and God in me' and that 'it is no longer I that live but God lives in me', and 'the works which I do are not my own but God who dwells in me does his works'.[8]

This universal mind, by reflecting on its own source, ultimately grows into the unitary mind in which the universal mind realizes its unity with the divine consciousness. In this level a person says, 'God and I are one' or 'God alone is'. The Upanishad sages declared this realization with the words 'I am Brahman (aham Brahma asmi). Jesus said, 'the Father and I are one'.[9] This level can be described as the mind of conscious unity or unitary consciousness. This is the seventh level of consciousness. In Hinduism they call it non-dualistic consciousness. In Buddhism they call it Dharmakaya, the Buddha nature. In this stage a person realizes that he/she has returned to the original stage, original home. It was there in the beginning but there was no awareness of it. At the beginning there was unity but it was unconscious. At the end there is the same unity but it is conscious. This is our spiritual evolution. We begin with unconscious unity and grow into conscious unity. In this process we go through different levels of minds or consciousnesses, which are the necessary outcome of the evolutionary process of human spiritual growth. The difficulty comes only when one stops somewhere on the way. Our spiritual journey is like climbing a hill. Our journey should lead us ultimately to the top of the hill and then bring us back to our starting point. But if we stop on the way and build a house there and settle down, then we stop our spiritual journey and live in a fragmented truth, which is the source of divisions, conflict and violence in the world.

The first level of the mind, which is unconscious unity and the last level of the mind, which is conscious unity, are one and the same. The only difference is that the first one is unconscious and the last one is conscious. The second level, which is unconscious mutual indwelling or unconscious universal mind, and the sixth one, which is conscious mutual indwelling or conscious universal mind, are one and the same. In both levels one lives by the life of God very intimately. But the only difference is that in the second level it is unconscious and in the sixth level it is conscious. The third level, the social mind and the fifth level, the mature individual mind, are the same. But in the social mind society imposes its ideals on an individual whereas in the mature individual mind an individual does the demands of society out of understanding—without the feeling of being imposed.

Between the first three levels and the last three levels is the fourth level, the rebellious individual mind, where an individual emerges. The birth of the individual mind is necessary for the evolution of human consciousness. There is no direct path from the unconscious unity to the conscious unity (except by the grace of God). In order to grow from the first three levels into the next three levels one has to become an individual. It is a narrow path one has to grow through. Jesus said, 'enter by the narrow gate'.[10] It is a narrow gate because only one person at a time can go through it. This narrow gate is the process of becoming an individual. It is like coming out of the womb of the social mind. Jesus told Nicodemus to come out of his religious womb in order to enter into the kingdom of heaven. If the social mind is aware of its limitations and opens human beings towards the unitary mind then there will not be much conflict between the social mind and the rebellious individual mind. But if the social mind thinks that it is absolute then there will be a conflict between the social mind and the individual mind.

In the social mind we encounter the God of authority and power, who demands the submission of will and intellect. In the universal mind we encounter the God of freedom and eternity, who gives back will and intellect to human beings. Jesus said, 'just as the Father has life in himself, he has granted the Son to have life in himself.[11] I have come to give life and give it abundantly'.[12] To have life within is to have love and freedom because love is freedom and freedom is life. God is life, love and freedom. He has given that freedom to Jesus and Jesus came to give that freedom abundantly to every human being. We grow from the God of authority into the God of freedom, from the God of words into the God of silence. If an individual mind remains only at the rebellious stage then society falls into extreme individualism and this can be dangerous to society. There will be a continuous conflict between social mind and an individual mind. Atheism and secularism are a kind of rebellion against the social God, the God of authority. They belong to the rebellious individual mind and can even belong to mature individual mind. If this stage is used positively then it can open human consciousness to the God of freedom.

Our Spiritual Evolution and the Story of the Garden of Eden

The story of the Garden of Eden explains, in a beautiful way, this evolution of human consciousness—but it does not tell it to the end.

Before God created the world and humanity, we can say they were one with God. There was unconscious unity. When God created (whatever that may mean) the world and humanity they were in the womb of God. It was as if God became pregnant with creation. Humanity was in the womb of God. The Garden of Eden was the womb of God. They had a very intimate relationship with God, as if they were living by the life of God, just as a fœtus lives by the life of a pregnant woman. It was an experience of unconscious mutual indwelling or unconscious universal mind. God lived in them and they lived in God. They were also like new-born children. They were naked and they were not ashamed. They did not know good and evil. They had an unconditioned mind. Then God told them that they could eat all the fruits in the garden except the fruit of good and evil. By telling them what they should do and should not do God became a social mind. God became a social authority, which demands the obedience of will and intellect. He told them what was right and what was wrong. When God told humanity what they should do and what they should not do then began the social mind. In the social mind they have lost their original innocence and original unity. At the same time the social mind gave some security and protection to human consciousness. Social mind was also an extended womb of God. The Garden of Eden extends up to the social mind because if a person obeys the social mind it gives protection from guilt and sin. The Garden of Eden embraces the unconscious unity, the unconscious mutual indwelling, and the social mind. But in these three levels there are no real individuals.

The Serpent

The desire to become like God is nothing but the desire to become conscious of our unconscious unity with God. It is not a bad desire. The desire to know good and evil is the desire to come out of the social authority of God and to have authority within oneself. The serpent seduced Adam and Eve to eat the fruit of good and evil so that they could become conscious of their unity with God. Good and evil, as duality, belong to the relative order. Since the desire to become like God is the desire to become conscious of our original unity with God, it is not something bad but projecting outside what is already within. We need to project outside what we are inside in order to realize it consciously. But by projecting what is within outside, humanity initiates duality, time, relative good and evil and distance between God and itself.

In their deepest level Adam and Eve were already like God, as they were created in the image and likeness of God–there was no need for them to become like God but they were not unconscious of the fact. They needed to become conscious of it. By eating the forbidden fruit they developed the rebellious individual mind. This eating of the forbidden fruit has two aspects: one is that it is a fall and the other is that it is a growth. It is a fall because it breaks the social mind. It falls from the social mind into individual mind. There is good in the social mind. When someone breaks the social mind that person is doing harm to himself and to society. But it is also growth because it is the birth of an individual. Here fall and growth coincide. Unless one becomes an individual spiritual evolution does not take place. Hence the serpent in the story, in a way, is helping human consciousness to come out of original innocence and move towards conscious unity. In this sense we can say that the serpent is also in the plan of God. But the serpent is not somewhere outside, it is within everyone. By projecting outside what is inside humanity also initiates the duality of good and evil. It seems it is a necessary and inevitable process. Adam and Eve, by rebelling against the social God, initiated the evolution of human consciousness from the God of authority to the God of freedom, from the God of history to the God of eternity. It was a very important stage in the evolution of human consciousness. It was a happy fault, Felix culpa.

The Gate with an Angel

After the fall, human beings find themselves outside the Garden of Eden. God closed the gate of the Garden and posted an angel with a sword in order that human beings may not enter the Garden.[13] The temptation for the human mind could be to regress when it faces difficulties: to go back into the social mind or unconscious universal mind instead of growing towards conscious unity. Humanity cannot regress it has to progress through suffering. Now human consciousness oscillates between the social mind and the rebellious individual mind. The social mind demands the individual come back to it whereas the individual mind rebels against the social mind. When we read the Old Testament we realize how often God calls his people 'rebellious and stiff-necked'! He calls people to return to him. It is an invitation to return to the Law, the social mind of God. The Law represents the social mind. This tension continues in the Jewish tradition until the coming of Christ. Prophets realized that there was no solution at the level of the social mind, the Law. They foresaw a new relationship with God in which the Law would be written in the hearts of the people. Prophet Jeremiah says, 'Behold the days are coming, when I make a new covenant with the people of Israel. I will write the law in the hearts of the people...'[14] This new covenant is the birth of universal mind, which in turn opens the door to the unitary mind.

The Spiritual Evolution of Jesus

We can see that in Jesus this spiritual evolution has reached its climax. We can say that Jesus began with unconscious unity with the Father. St. John says, 'in the beginning was the word, the word was with God and the word was God. The word became flesh'.[15] In the womb of Mary he was in the unconscious universal mind. At the moment of his circumcision he entered into the social mind of Judaism. As he realized slowly the limitations of his spiritual tradition he entered into the rebellious individual mind. He was considered to be a rebel by the Jewish spiritual authorities. He became a rebel to his social system and acquired a mature mind, which opened him to surrender to the divine at the moment of his baptism. The heavens were opened and the spirit of God came upon him and he heard the voice of God, 'You are my beloved son'.[16] In this experience he realized what his real nature was and that became the light through which he had to live his life. There was no more external social mind, the Law. Now he would say, 'I am in the Father and the Father is in me'.[17] 'The works which I do are not my own but the Father who dwells in me does his work'.[18] It is an experience of conscious mutual indwelling. He was in God and God in him. He was in the womb of God and was living by the life of God, just like a foetus lives by the life of a pregnant woman. In this experience Jesus inaugurated the new covenant promised by God through the prophets. In the new covenant a person declares: 'I am the way, the truth and the life'.

He did not remain there but went one step further and experienced that he and his Father were one. He declared, 'The Father and I are one'.[19] In this sense Jesus completed the evolutionary process of human spiritual growth. The unconscious original unity became conscious unity in him. From this realization onwards he said that he was one with God from the beginning, that he came from the Father, that he and the Father were one and he would go back to the Father.

But this experience or realization is not limited to Jesus alone. Jesus has made this a blueprint of the spiritual journey for every human being. Every human being begins with unconscious unity and has to return to conscious unity. The divisions in the name of truth can come only when people remain either at the social mind (religions belong to the social mind), or at the rebellious individual mind, or at the mature mind. Only in the universal mind and in the unitary mind do all the divisions disappear. This evolution of Jesus is also an evolution in love of God and love of neighbour. It is an evolution from individual love to collective love, from collective love to universal love and from universal to divine love.

Spiritual Evolution and Free Will

It is common to say in the Prophetic religions that God created human beings with free will and intellect. One really needs to reflect on this issue.

The author's contention is that God did not create human beings with free will and intellect but that free will and intellect belong to the evolutionary process of human consciousness. It is not there at the beginning and it will not be there at the end. In between it comes and disappears. When we look at the different levels of consciousness described above we see this very clearly.

In the first stage of unconscious unity there is no free will and intellect. It is the level of the absolute freedom of God. In the second stage of unconscious mutual indwelling (pre-social mind) there is no free will or intellect either. Here a person completely lives by the life of God. He or she reflects the absolute goodness of God.

In the third stage of social mind there is will and intellect but they are not free because they have to conform to the social will and social intellect. In the Garden of Eden when God told humanity 'do this and do not do that', there is no free choice. They have to obey the voice of God because there is only one voice and one authority. In order to make a choice we need two voices or two authorities. But in the social mind there is only one voice and one has to obey it. Hence in the social mind there is free will but this will is conditioned by the society in which a person lives. There is a possibility to make a free choice only if we have two equal voices. Adam and Eve in order to make a choice had to create two voices: the voice of God and the voice of the serpent. If one reflects very clearly there is no choice to be made because these two voices are not equal: one is the creator and the other is a creature. In order to make a choice between these two voices either one has to elevate the serpent to the level of God or bring down God to the level of the serpent. When we do this we create two equal authorities, between which we choose to choose. We can say that the fall of humanity is a fall from non-duality into duality. It is a fall from one absolute reality to two absolute realities.

In the fourth level of rebellious mind, free will and intellect emerge. Individuals being freed from the social mind begin to think independently and even critically of the social mind, represented by parents, religion and social customs. They enter into conflict with the social mind. They begin to make independent choices. Here the person's choices are based on individual needs and fulfilment. The whole morality will be based on individualism. In this level the society revolves around individualism. An individual is the centre and the society is at the service of the individual (in the social mind the individual is at the service of the society). Present European society reflects this rebellious and individual mind. The emergence of this rebellious mind is very important for the evolution of human consciousness even though it is limited and has negative consequences. This is the narrow path one has to grow through. It is like the birth of a baby from the womb of social mind. It is a painful process both for society and the individual. This is the door that opens the human consciousness to the fifth level of consciousness–the mature individual mind.

In the fifth level (mature individual mind) will and intellect exist but they are mature; they are not controlled from the outside. Such individuals realize the interconnectedness of human beings and their own responsibility towards others. Every action is seen in its effect over others. We can say that ideologies like socialism and humanism are born from this mature mind. Even though a person is thinking freely this person's thinking is conditioned by the others and their needs. There is respect and concern for others; it is not self-centred or fanatic. It is reasonable, open to listen and open to receive corrections. Even though it is mature, yet we cannot say that it has real free will. Its will and intellect are somehow conditioned. Only in the sixth level, in the Universal mind, a person can have real free will.

In the sixth level (universal mind) there is no essential free will and there is no essential intellect. The individual will and intellect merge with the universal will and intellect. By surrendering one's will and intellect one enters into inner freedom. One lives and acts from inner freedom. The individual will and intellect have functional value and become the vehicle of the universal will and intellect. This universal will and intellect is the reflection of the divine will. Here one's will becomes God's will. This is the experience of the new covenant promised by God. It is the law written in the heart. No one will tell another to know God but everyone knows God. And there is no remembrance of any sin. There is sin in the individual will and in the collective will but in the universal will there is no sin. Because in the universal will God is the actor and God's actions are always righteous. This universal will finally merges into the unitary will of God. At this seventh level there is only freedom: human will and intellect are the vehicles of the divine will–they have no essential value but only functional value. Jesus said, 'the Father has granted all authority to the Son. The son does what he sees his Father doing'.[20]

Hence we can say that human will and intellect have their beginning in the social mind, grow through rebellious and mature minds and then come to an end in the universal mind and the unitary mind. In the evolutionary process they look as if they are essential but in the universal mind they become only functional. They are not at the beginning and they will not be at the end. To be at the level of the will and the intellect is to be in the realm of conflict. Only by surrendering our will and intellect (by outgrowing them) we find ultimate peace and joy in our life. It is in this context we have to understand the prayer of Jesus when he says, 'Not my will, let thy will be done'.[21] Only at the level of conscious unity do we find our ultimate fulfilment. When Jesus said, 'unless you become like little children, you cannot enter into the kingdom of God',[22] he was referring to this spiritual journey. Children do not have will and intellect. They are innocent and ignorant. They are in an unconscious bliss.

But we have to become like children consciously. It is not regressing but growing into conscious bliss. Thus the author contends that God did not create human beings with free will and intellect; rather God created them with inner freedom together with the possibility of acquiring will and intellect in their evolution towards the conscious unity. Free will and intellect are not at the beginning and they will not be at the end. In the social mind, rebellious mind and mature individual minds, will and intellect are there, very much conditioned, but in the universal mind and in the unitary mind they are unconditioned. They are at the service of inner freedom. Only where there is inner freedom can we speak of real free will and intellect, otherwise our will and intellect are always conditioned. Hence our spiritual evolution is from conditioned will to unconditioned free will or freedom.

Spiritual Evolution and the Problem of Evil

What is the source of Evil? If God is absolute good where does Evil come from? There cannot be an absolute Evil in opposition to God. If there is then we fall into dualism of two Gods: good God and evil God. But there is only one God and this one God is absolute good. If so where does evil come from? When we speak about evil we are speaking of relative evil and not absolute evil which does not exist. When we look at the different levels of consciousness in our spiritual evolution the place of evil becomes clear. Just as we have seen in the above that the will and intellect belong to the evolutionary process of human consciousness so also we can say that (moral) evil belongs to the evolutionary process of human consciousness. In the first level of unconscious unity there is no evil. There is no duality of good and evil. There is only the absolute goodness of God. In the second level of unconscious mutual indwelling there is no good and evil but only the reflection of the absolute goodness of God. In the third level of social mind there is relative good and relative evil. Here, good is everything that is in conformity with the social mind and evil is that which is against the social mind. In the rebellious individual mind there is relative good and relative evil. This good and evil depends on each individual. There is also relative good and relative evil in the mature individual mind since it is also limited but this good and evil are connected to social responsibility. There is no good and evil in the universal mind. There is only the reflection of the absolute goodness of God. In the conscious unitary mind there is only absolute Good. So there is no duality of good and evil at the level of unconscious unity, in unconscious mutual indwelling, the universal mind and the unitary mind. There is relative good and evil in the social mind, in the rebellious individual mind and in the mature individual mind. It begins in the social mind and comes to an end in the universal mind, just as the will and the intellect begin with the social mind and come to an end in the universal mind.

Will and evil are very much connected. Where there is fragmented will there is good and evil. It is the fragmented will and intellect which are the source of relative good and relative evil. God told humanity not to eat the fruit of good and evil. To eat the fruit of good and evil is to fall into fragmented will and intellect: it is the desire to know good and evil and the desire to make a choice. Since this advice was given when human consciousness was still in its unconscious universal mind and that advice initiates social mind, there would be a fascination for the social mind to be attracted by the fruit of good and evil. It has to loose its social mind and enter into the individual mind in order to begin its journey to the conscious unity. The serpent seduced human consciousness to come out the womb of the social mind and put it on the path to conscious unity. To go beyond good and evil is to go beyond individual will and intellect and social will and intellect. It is to go beyond duality, to go beyond choices where our choices become choice-less choices. They come from inner freedom. We have to grow in our spiritual life in such a way that we come to a point where we are able to say sincerely, 'not my will, let thy will be done.'[23] In the new covenant a person goes beyond good and evil. There is no remembrance of any sin. It is to re-enter the Garden of Eden, where there is no consciousness of good and evil but manifesting the absolute freedom and goodness of God.

Our Spiritual Evolution and the Parable of the Prodigal Son

The parable of the prodigal son[24] is another beautiful description of the spiritual journey of humanity from unconscious unity to conscious unity. This parable fulfils the story of the Garden of Eden. It certainly is not a story about one young man but the story of every human being. The prodigal son was one with the father before he was born. After his birth he had an unconscious mutual indwelling with his Father. What belonged to his father belonged to him. He entered into the social mind when he tried to fulfil the demands of his father. Then he rebelled against his father (social mind) by demanding his share of property: it was the emergence of his individuality. It was the rebellious mind. He became an individual and spent his life fulfilling his personal desires and ambitions. But he did not find fulfilment in it. He realized his mistake. He repented and came to a mature mind. He came back to his father and entered into the universal mind. He experienced the unconditional love of God. What belonged to his father belonged to him and from there we suppose he entered into the unitary mind. The elder son remained in the social mind. He did not become an individual. We can say that the younger son had a more mature relationship with his father than the elder son. The scribes and the Pharisees, the so-called righteous people were like the elder son. The tax collectors, the prostitutes and the sinners were like the younger son. They were in the rebellious mind. Jesus told the scribes and the Pharisees that the tax collectors, the prostitutes and the sinners were entering the kingdom before them. He also taught that one has to transcend the righteousness of the scribes and the Pharisees in order to enter into the kingdom. It is to go beyond the social mind, beyond the rebellious mind and beyond the mature mind. It is to enter into the universal mind. The parable of the prodigal son completes and fulfils the story of the Garden of Eden. The story of the Garden of Eden stops with the rebellious individual mind. The parable of the prodigal son brings humanity back to the original unity, returns to the original harmony but with consciousness. The story of the Garden of Eden did not happen in the past, it is happening again and again. Whenever a child is born the Garden of Eden is beginning. The child is in the unconscious universal mind. It has to grow into the conscious unity.

The Tree of Life

The tree of life is the tree of unity. Though it is divided into roots, trunk, and branches and leaves it is still one. The leaves are aware of their connectedness to the branches, the branches are aware of their connectedness to the trunk and the trunk is aware of its dependence on the roots. There is only one tree, one life, one truth and one way, the way of the tree. The same life is flowing in every part of the tree. There is only absolute Good. There is no good and evil.

The Tree of Good and Evil

The tree of good and evil is the tree where there is fragmentation of truth. In the first level leaves do not recognize their dependency on the branches. Each leaf wants to be an authority in itself. Each leaf wants to live for itself. Human consciousness falls into extreme individualism. Here truth is reduced to individualism. Hinduism calls it the Kali Yuga, where truth walks on one foot only. Each leaf wants to relate with the roots directly, without a branch and the trunk. It may even deny the existence of the roots.

In the second level, each leaf recognizes the existence of the branches and its dependence on them. Some leaves are attached to a branch and think that their branch has the absolute truth. They do not recognize the truth existing in the other branches. They see evil in the other branches. Here truth is reduced into ideals or collective consciousness. Individuals are under the guidance of ideals and ideal persons. Here truth walks on two legs. Hinduism calls it the Dwapara Yuga; Dwapara means two. It is the age of duality. Each branch tries to relate with the roots directly without the trunk.

In the third level the leaves realize that the branches are dependent on the trunk and the trunk holds all the branches and the leaves together nourishing them with the nutrition received form the roots. The awareness grows into the trunk. The trunk is the mediator between roots and branches and leaves. There the truth walks on three legs. Hinduism calls it the Treta Yuga; Treta means three. It is the age of the universal mind.

In the fourth level human consciousness enters into roots and realizes its unity with God. There the truth walks on four legs. It is fullness of truth. Hinduism calls it the Sathya Yuga, the age of truth.

In the Kali Yuga and the Dwapar Yuga human beings have dualistic relationship with God. They think of themselves as creatures of God. In the Treta Yuga, human beings experience themselves as the sons and daughters of God. They have the experience of the indwelling presence of God. In the Sathya Yuga human beings realize themselves as one with God. A person says 'God and I are one' or 'God alone is'. God is the whole tree. She/he is the roots, the trunk, the branches and the leaves. He or she is everything.

To eat the fruit from the tree of good and evil is to fall from unity into duality, from wholeness into fragmentation, from fullness into emptiness, from the absolute goodness into relative good and relative evil, from freedom into conditioned free will, from one truth into many truths, from one way into many ways, from peace into conflict, from joy into suffering. To eat the fruit from the tree of life is to reverse this process. It is to move from duality to non-duality, from fragmentation to wholeness, from relative goodness and evil to absolute goodness, from conditioned free will to freedom or free will, from many truths to one truth, from many ways to one way, from conflict and violence to peace, from suffering to joy.

In the Biblical tradition the story of the Garden of Eden describes the evolutionary process of human consciousness but it does not complete it. The author who wrote it was in dualistic consciousness. Jesus completed this process in the parable of the prodigal son. Jesus was in non-dualistic consciousness. Hence the spiritual evolution of human consciousness is from Unconscious Unity to Conscious Unity, from Free will to Freedom. In the Biblical tradition Jesus Christ is the blue print of this spiritual evolution, which every human being is invited to realize in his or her life spiritual journey.

4.
IN THE FOOTPRINTS OF VIRGIN MARY

We are living in a very difficult time. It is a difficult time for God, a difficult time for Religions, a difficult time for Christianity, a difficult time for the Catholic Church, a difficult time for religious life, a difficult time for monastic life and a difficult time for individuals wishing to choose a way of life.

It is a difficult time for God because the atheists and secularists have declared the death of God and consider that those who believe in God are in God-delusion. They have become as much missionaries as theists were before them and they have determined to remove God from the public life by all means.

Every crisis is an invitation to reform, to purify and to grow. If we do not respond to a crisis in a positive and adequate way then we will degenerate and fall into self-destruction. Today the Roman Catholic Church is in a deep crisis particularly in the developed countries. She needs a healing touch, she needs a way out. When I say: healing the Catholic Church, I also mean healing myself since I am also a part of that Church.

Scientific advancement, secularization and relativism in the developed countries have contributed in the drastic drop in church attendance. Even in Ireland, within twenty years, church attendance has descended to 5 to 10 per cent from 85 per cent. Vocations to the priesthood and religious life have reached the lowest and many monasteries and religious orders are closing down due to lack of vocations. Many priests have to take care of more than one parish. The church does not see anything positive in secularism and relativism but tries to combat it. Over and above secularism and relativism, clerical sexual abuse and mistreatment of children under the care of the educational institutions of the Church has caused tremendous damage to the children, to the families of the children, to the ordinary believer and to the Church hierarchy. It continues to be a source of sadness and shame.

The faithful are angry at the injustice done to children and they look at the Church with repulsion. The leadership in the church feels guilty for what happened. The leadership not only did not protect the children but also covered up the abuse at an official level. There is a great shock and dismay in the hierarchy for what happened to innocent children. Those who were supposed to protect the children abused the children. Like the proverbial 'fence eating the crop'. The wounds arising from this abuse cannot be healed so easily.

At the same time one has to be aware that the Church is not only those who have abused the children and those who have covered it up but also those great saints and martyrs who have born great witness to the love of God manifested in Christ; those priests and religious who have heroically dedicated their lives for the love of God, and all the believers who are faithful to the teachings of Christ. In moments of despair and hopelessness we need to look at them for courage and hope. Particularly we need to look to Christ, the source of our faith, for support, healing and inspiration.

Today we stand between the two camps: the faithful who are shocked to know what happened and have lost faith, confidence and trust in the Church as an institution; and the leadership that is stunned to discover the terrible stories of child abuse and their cover-up and does not know how to proceed. On the part of the leadership there is a need for genuine conversion, repentance and seeking forgiveness from the Lord and from the abused; and on the part of the abused there is a need to receive the healing touch from the Lord and receive the capacity to forgive those who have abused them. It is not very easy to forgive those who have caused such deep wounds, which affected people's entire lives. Christ is our only model. He has forgiven the genuine sinners and bestowed unconditional love. He also asked God to forgive those who have humiliated him by killing him like a criminal on the cross.

At the same time it is not sufficient that we forgive and forget and get on as usual as if nothing had happened; there must be a renewal, a reformation, a growth and even a revolution. Every crisis has two possibilities: either we go upwards or we go downwards. We do not remain the same. For this we need to kneel down and pray sincerely and open our hearts and minds to listen to the inspirations of the Holy Spirit, to listen to what the Holy Spirit wants to tell us today. We need to go back to the first inspiration of our religion, Jesus Christ, and see what would be his answer for the crisis we are in now. We need to reflect on his vision and see how it can help us to come out of the present crisis.

Jesus Christ came to bear witness to the Kingdom of God. He proclaimed the kingdom of God and invited his listeners to discover this kingdom. This kingdom experience was a revolution in his life. It is a transition from the spirituality centred on religion to the spirituality that is centred on God. It is the inauguration of the new covenant that

God promised to the people of Israel: 'the Lord says, the time is coming when I will make a new covenant with the people of Israel and with the people of Judah. It will not be like the old covenant that I made with their ancestors when I took them by the hand and led them out of Egypt. Although I was like a husband to them, they did not keep that covenant. The new covenant that I will make with the people of Israel will be this: I will put my law within them and write it on their hearts. I will be their God and they will be my people. None of them will have to teach his fellow countryman to know the Lord, because all will know me, from the least to the greatest. I will forgive their sins and I will no longer remember their wrongs. I the Lord have spoken'.[25]

In spirituality centred on religion, religion comes first, second comes God as understood by that religion and third come human beings who have to worship God in that religion. In this stage religion is greater than human beings and human beings serve religion. God is experienced as the God of authority who demands the submission of will and intellect and absolute loyalty. Religious leaders have power over the followers. In spirituality centred on God, first comes God, who is greater than human beings and religions, second come human beings who, in their deepest level, are greater than religions and third comes religion which is meant to be at the service of human beings. Here God is experienced as the God of freedom and silence. This is the revolution that Jesus brought through his experience of the kingdom. This is the spirituality of the new covenant.

The Kingdom of God is the spirituality centred on God, not on religion. Jesus said that 'the Sabbath is made for human beings and not human beings for the sake of the Sabbath'[26]. We can substitute the word 'religion' for Sabbath. Religion is made to be at the service of human beings and not human beings at the service of religion. Jesus also said 'do not think that I have come to abolish the Law and the Prophets; I have not come to abolish them but to fulfil them'[27]. Again we can substitute the word 'religion' for the Law. He did not come to abolish religions but to fulfil them for they are also in the plan of God. The first covenant, in which God gave Ten Commandments to Moses, instituted a religion with rituals, morality and authority. In the second covenant, the New Covenant, God writes the Law of love within everyone's heart. In fact it is not writing something newly but revealing what is already there in everyone's heart. God has written his eternal covenant in the heart of every human being as he or she is born. In the new covenant God reveals to people who they are and not what they should or should not do.

Jesus told the Samaritan woman that in the future people would worship God no more in the temples or mountains but in spirit and truth. 'But the hour is coming, and is now here, when the true worshipers will worship the Father in spirit and truth, for the Father is seeking such people to worship him. God is spirit, and those who worship him must worship in spirit and truth'.[28] This is the new covenant. In the first covenant a person will say that religion is the way, the truth and the life and in the new covenant a person will say 'I am the way, the truth and the life'[29] But one cannot start with the new covenant. One has to grow in the first covenant then only can one move into the new. We can say that the first covenant is the womb of God. God protects, nourishes and gives security to the people in the Law and then when people are fully grown he gives birth to them into the freedom of the kingdom of God. The new covenant is the fulfilment of the Law and the Prophets. Jesus made this transition into the new covenant at the moment of his baptism. He invited his listeners to do the same.

Jesus was angry with the religious leaders of his time. He said, 'woe to you, scribes and Pharisees, hypocrites, for you lock the people out of the kingdom of heaven; neither you enter nor allow others to enter.'[30] The scripture has the keys to open the door to the new covenant. But the religious leaders neither used them for themselves nor allowed others to use them. They were in spiritual bondage and held people in spiritual bondage. Jesus used these keys and opened the door to the kingdom of God, for his own spiritual growth and for the growth of all human beings. He gave these keys to his disciples for their spiritual growth. He asked them to help others in their spiritual evolution. But unfortunately his followers have misinterpreted this message and transformed these keys into the keys of power and authority and held people in the same spiritual bondage without knowing what they were doing. They did not take the spiritual evolution forward. Their only progress: they accepted that Christ could evolve in this manner, but they denied that they or others might do so. If Jesus comes today he will say the same to the Church leaders: 'I have given you the keys to the kingdom of God, to the new covenant, but you neither entered it nor allowed others to enter it. You remained in the first covenant and kept others also in it'. Jesus Christ had opened the door to the new covenant but unfortunately Christianity closed it again very soon even though unconsciously.

We also have the episode of Virgin Mary and Herod.

Herod is the symbol of an institution that wants power, position and continuity. Herod wants children only for his continuity. He does not want any child who can be a threat to his position, power and continuity. It means that for all the children, even before their birth, Herod has already decided that they are going to be at his service. They have no life of their own. It is for this reason Herod is called the murderer of innocent children. Any child who can be a threat to his position will be killed. He is alert, cunning and ruthless.

Virgin Mary is the symbol of an institution that gives birth to children for God. She is cooperating with the plan of God. She has no desire for power, position and continuity. Her only desire is to rear children for God. She looks at her own son as the Son of God and worships him. She is like a nanny for God's children. She is at God's service. She is powerless and vulnerable. She is one hundred per cent dependent on God's providence. She gave birth to a child who will take away the power of Herod and give life to all the children. Virgin Mary was giver of life and Jesus also was giver of life.

Herod wants children only for himself, to worship him. Herod can give protection, sustenance and security but only if people accept his power and authority. He is like a cage. People are imprisoned within the cage and the keys are in his hands. They survive but cannot grow.

Virgin Mary is like a nest in which people are born, protected, nourished and given security until they are ready to move into the freedom of the kingdom of God. The purpose of any religion, as institution, is to nourish its followers in its nest and prepare them to fly into the freedom of the kingdom of God. A religion with its belief structures is like a womb of God. It has to conceive and nourish; and when the time comes it needs to give birth to its children into freedom. If it does not want to do that then the womb becomes a tomb. People enter a religion but never come out. They die there. Religion becomes Herod, killing innocent children in its womb. Spiritual evil can be described as that which blocks the spiritual evolution of human beings.

The Church began her journey as Virgin Mary. She was fragile, vulnerable and powerless and suffered under many Herods. But very soon she turned into Herod when she was established as a state religion. She gives security, protection and sustenance to her followers but only if they obey her. She wants to keep everyone in her womb. She never delivers them into freedom. Anyone who is a threat to her power and position will be ruthlessly eliminated.

The greatness of any religion does not depend on how many followers it has in its womb but how many followers it has given birth to into the freedom of the infinite sky. Secularism and atheism should be seen as the profound aspirations of people to escape the cage of Herod and fly into the freedom of the kingdom of God. They belong to the evolutionary process of human spiritual growth. They reveal the desire of the human consciousness to discover the new covenant, the truth within. The Catholic Church needs to open its spirituality to satisfy the aspirations of secularism and atheism. Its spirituality should embrace not only those who are within its four walls but also outside of them.

The crisis in which the Catholic Church finds itself now may be the right moment for it to transforms itself again into Virgin Mary and to give birth to children for God and not for itself. Jesus Christ was similar to Mary in wanting to give birth to children for God, not for himself. The Church should follow the example of its founder who washed the feet of his disciples as a sign that he had come to facilitate the spiritual growth of human beings and not to control them. It is not sufficient to do this symbolic ceremony on Maundy Thursday once a year: it should be a real daily service. It means that the Church has to renounce its desire for power, control and position. It should be humble like Mary.

Herod without desire for power becomes Virgin Mary. A cage without a door becomes a nest. Jesus wants his Church to be a nest and a mother-bird. It is there only to protect, nourish and give security until people are ready to take the plunge into the freedom of the kingdom of God. This is the radical change or conversion that Jesus Christ demands from his Church. This is also one way through which the Church can come out of her present crisis and become a nurturing religion, a liberating religion as intended by her teacher and master, Jesus Christ.

5.
JOURNEY TO THE INNER JERUSALEM

Spiritual life is a journey. It is a journey from God outside to God inside, from the Law to the Kingdom of God, from Moses to Christ, from the Old (first) Covenant to the New Covenant, from external Temple to inner Temple, from external Jerusalem to inner Jerusalem.

In the gospel of Luke[31] Jesus was going with his disciples towards Jerusalem, the city of God, to bear witness to the truth that he has discovered or realized. He was aware that the truth he would proclaim would certainly provoke conflict with the religious authorities there. But he was ready for it. On the way Jesus had to pass through a Samaritan village. The Samaritans did not want to receive him because he was going towards Jerusalem; probably they thought that he might proclaim the supremacy of Jerusalem, which the Samaritans did not recognize. We may remember what the Samaritan woman told Jesus: 'our fathers worshipped on this mountain though you (the Jews) say that Jerusalem is the place where one ought to worship'.[32] We may remember also Jesus' answer to the Samaritan woman when he said that in the future 'you will worship the Father neither on this mountain nor in Jerusalem but in spirit and truth. God is spirit and those who worship must worship in spirit and truth'.[33]

So Jesus was certainly not going to Jerusalem to proclaim the supremacy of Jerusalem but inviting people to discover the divine within, to worship God in spirit and truth. He was going there to open the door to the New Jerusalem, the inner Jerusalem, which is the heart of every human being. This message will make the Law and the Temple relative. This would certainly put him in conflict with the Jewish religious authorities and would provoke refusal and violence.

Jesus Christ proclaimed the good news of the kingdom of God. This kingdom was something that Jesus found or discovered in his life. The kingdom experience was a fulfilment and revolution in his life. Jesus began his ministry with the words, 'the kingdom of God is at hand, repent'.[34] He also said, 'first of all seek you the kingdom of God and its righteousness and all things will be given unto you.'[35] His mission was to invite people to discover the kingdom of God, to lead people to the experience of the kingdom of God. The primary purpose of our existence as human beings, as Christians, as religious, as monks, nuns and lay-people is to search for the kingdom of God and its way of living. This is valid for all times: in the past, in the present and in the future. Only the situations and the context in which this search is made will always be new.

We take Jerusalem as the symbol of the kingdom of God, the New Jerusalem, the inner Jerusalem, our permanent home.

We have three types of homes. The first one is the physical home that is connected to the needs of our physical bodies. It is an external structure. The second type is the ideological homes, our belief structures and ways of living. The third is the eternal home, the kingdom of God that transcends physical and ideological homes. Jesus said that 'the foxes have their holes, the birds have their nests but the son of man has nowhere to lie down and rest'. He was not speaking of a physical home but of an ideological home. He was living in the eternal home.

The eternal home does not exclude the ideological and physical homes but includes them and transcends them. It is like the infinite space. This eternal home, the kingdom of God, is the ultimate destiny of our spiritual evolution. Jesus wants to lead everyone to the kingdom of God, to the inner Jerusalem.

Jesus did not define what 'the kingdom of God' is but he did describe it in a number of ways. The kingdom of God is the discovery of the unconditional love of God, like the sun that shines on both the good and the bad. It is the experience of the radical love of God and the radical love of neighbour. Jesus described this with two statements: the father and I are one'[36] and 'whatever you do to the least of my brothers and sisters that you do unto me'.[37] The first one reveals the radical love of God and the second one reveals the radical love of neighbour. It transforms all our actions into actions of God. It is dying to ourselves in such a way that our emptiness becomes a space for God to complete his/her works. Jesus said that 'the works that I do are not my own but the father who dwells in me does his works'.[38]

The kingdom of God is discovering our deepest reality that manifests in time and space, but has its foundation in eternity. This deepest reality escapes all our labels and it can only say, 'I am'. Jesus often used this expression 'I am'. Jesus said that the kingdom of God is like a man who found treasure in a field.[39] He went home sold everything and bought that field. The kingdom of God is like a merchant in search of pearls.[40] When he finds a pearl of great value he goes home, sells everything and buys that pearl. The kingdom of God is to discover our eternal self, our eternal 'I am', which is our image and likeness of God. The kingdom of God is returning to our home, where we find rest, relax and feel comfortable. Jesus said, 'come to me all you who labour and are over-burdened, I will give you rest. Take my yoke upon you and learn from me for I am meek and humble of heart and you will find rest for your souls. For my yoke is easy and my burden is light.'[41]

The kingdom of God is also participating at the divine banquet.[42] It is a banquet in which God offers himself/herself as food to human beings and human beings offer themselves as food to God. It is a banquet of transformation, a banquet of spiritual alchemy in which divine becomes human and human become divine. Jesus said that 'the kingdom of God is like a woman who took yeast and placed it in three measures of flour until it was leavened'. The flour is our human nature and the leaven is divine life. Our human nature is penetrated by divine life. Jesus invited everyone to the banquet of the kingdom of God.

The kingdom of God is the inauguration of the new covenant in which God writes the Law of love in the heart of every human being. This is not really a new covenant, more an 'eternal covenant', for it is written in the heart of every human being. God does not write newly but makes human beings remember who they really are. It is coming back home. This is what happened to Jesus at the moment of his baptism. God told him, 'you are my beloved son'. This is writing the Law of Love in the heart of Jesus. For Jesus, it is also remembering who he really is. It is a kind of awakening, waking up from sleep and dreams. Jesus inaugurated this new covenant at the moment of his baptism. The kingdom of God is worshipping God in spirit and truth. Jesus invited his listeners to enter into this kingdom. How does one enter into this kingdom?

The Way–the Journey

The way that Jesus proposed is one but he described it varyingly, such as: repentance, to be born again, to become like little children, to lose oneself in order to find oneself, to die in order to be fruitful and to grow like a seed into a tree.

Jesus began his ministry with the words, 'the kingdom of God is at hand, repent'.[43] He told Nicodemus, 'unless you are born again, you cannot enter into the kingdom of heaven'.[44] He admonished his disciples, 'unless you become like little children, you cannot enter into the kingdom of heaven'.[45] Jesus said, 'if you lose your (limited) self, you will gain your (higher self); if you gain or cling to your (lower) self, you will lose your higher self.'[46] Jesus also said, 'unless a grain of wheat falls into the ground and dies, it remains alone but when it dies it gives a mighty harvest'.[47] He described the kingdom of God with a parable: 'the kingdom of God is like a mustard seed. It is the smallest of all seeds but when it grows it becomes so big that the birds of the air will come and make their nests in it'.[48] They are different ways of describing this one way. Repentance or conversion is not one simple act but it is a journey, a life-long journey. It is a continuous process of inner purification, inner growth. It is returning to our home; it is remembering our original self; it is to wake up; it is discovering the law written in our hearts; it is coming to the divine banquet, to the banquet of transformation, to the banquet of spiritual alchemy; it is transforming all our actions into actions of God and our life into the life of God.

Repentance is also going through a narrow gate, a narrow path. It is a necessary path one has to take. Jesus said, 'enter by the narrow gate'.[49] It is a narrow door because only one person can go through it at a time, like a child that comes out of the womb of its mother. It is a painful process but a necessary process. No one can do it for others. Others can only be like midwives to facilitate this transition. Each one has to take his/her cross and respond to the invitation of Jesus. It is the path of interiority. This journey is happening inside and not outside.

This interior journey has seven important moments or layers to it, not in an absolute sense but tentatively.

The first one is trying to live in one's own home or belief structure with sincerity and honesty. For Christians it is trying to follow the Ten Commandments given by God to Moses. It is the starting point. The second one is realizing the limitations of one's own home or belief structure. It is coming to the door, to the threshold. It is a condition in which our minds are not satisfied with the images of God and of ourselves transmitted to us through our tradition. We see their limitations. We see the difficulties in following them. Our minds become empty. We are at the threshold. The third moment is coming out of the door. It is leaving behind all our securities of home or village and entering into the insecurity of the desert. It is going through the narrow gate. The home or the village and the desert here are symbolic. This emptiness can be a barren emptiness where nothing grows, like the womb of Elizabeth. Elizabeth was barren without any hope. It is very difficult to be in that hopeless situation. But it is in this situation that John the Baptist is born. It is here that we encounter John the Baptist. It is here we receive the glimpses of hope. Elizabeth gives birth to hope. John the Baptist invites us beyond the village into the desert but points us beyond himself. He points us to Christ, to eternity, to the fullness of light.

The fourth moment is to make this barren womb or emptiness into a fertile womb or fertile emptiness, where life can be born. It is becoming like the womb of Mary. Mary's womb was empty but fertile, ready to give birth to life. Our minds become virgin minds, like minds of newborn children that are unconditioned but with infinite possibilities. Here we encounter Virgin Mary. It is here that our virgin minds hear the voice of Archangel Gabriel, who says 'blessed are you, because the God of Eternity, the God of now, 'I am who I am', wants to be born in you'. It is here we tremble with awe, fear and unworthiness. With awe because we are in the direct presence of God, the tremendous mystery and fascination. With fear because we are called to discontinue the God of the past, the God of Abraham, of Isaac and of Jacob. With the feeling of unworthiness. It is here we acclaim in disbelief: how is it possible that I am counted worthy of this grace? How can I handle this extraordinary grace, this extraordinary call, this extraordinary process? How can I convince others to accept this new life, this new message?

It is here that we discover the ultimate purpose of our human existence: to give birth to God–to transform all our actions into actions of God. It is also here that we discover that we have no choice but to say 'yes' to God because to say 'yes' to God is to say 'yes' to our own truth. It is the moment of great surrender: 'I am the handmaid of the Lord. Let it happen to me according to your will'. It is in this surrender that the spirit of God descends on us. It is like a seed that enters into the womb of a woman. Saint Peter says that we have the seed of God in us. It is accepting the seed of God, the spirit of God. We conceive the child of God. We become mothers of God. We say that our children are not our children but God's children; our actions are not our actions but God's actions. It is here that we encounter Mary; we enter into the consciousness of Mary. But Mary does not hold us to herself but points us to Christ, the fullness of truth. We need to move on.

In the fifth moment we renounce even the identity of being the mothers of God. Our consciousness enters into the heart of God and realizes that God alone is. We enter into the stage before we were created or manifested. It is here that we encounter Christ who says: 'the Father and I are one'.[50] It is here that we enter into the consciousness of Jesus. It is here we hear the words of Saint John, 'in the beginning was the Word; the Word was with God and the Word was God'.[51] This is discovering the kingdom of God, our permanent home.

That is the end of the ascending aspect of our conversion or repentance. This journey is entirely the work of grace. But we need also to make our descending journey. We need to come back to the awareness that we are physical beings with our needs and limitations.

The sixth moment is to encounter the Devil, the spirit of purification. In the process of returning we need to encounter the Devil. It will help us purify all the illusions we might have created from our spiritual experiences. It will test if we have any subtle ambitions of power, of position and of wealth. It will test if we feel that we are superior to others, if we feel we are better than others. It will help us to realize that having spiritual experiences does not give us any privileges. One is called to be a humble servant of God and his people.

The seventh moment is coming back to our spiritual home. It is here we recognize that the Law of Moses is still valid; it is our spiritual nest. Jesus said, 'I have not come to abolish the Law but to fulfil the Law'.[52] The kingdom of God does not abolish the Law but fulfils it.

Returning to our original home, to our original village, to the ordinary life is as difficult as moving into the desert. It is also a narrow path. It signifies dis-identifying with all the spiritual experiences that we have had and to come back to normality. Saint Paul says of Jesus: 'though being in the form of God Jesus did not count equality with God, a thing to be grasped, but he humbled himself and became obedient unto death, even death on a cross.'[53] Jesus had to encounter the Devil, the spirit of purification, before he returned to the village, to the market place.

The ordinary life is living a life of gratitude towards God and to all our brothers and sisters. It is a life of humility in service. It is washing the feet of our brothers and sisters. It is to say like Jesus that, 'the works which I do are not my own but the father who dwells in me does his works' and 'I have not come to be served but to serve'. When we say this we are in the kingdom of God. We are grounded in our permanent and eternal home. This is the destiny of every human being. It is the New Jerusalem, the inner Jerusalem, to which everyone will come ultimately to see God, Yahweh, and to which Jesus leads all his followers. Since Jesus himself went through this way he becomes our guide. He becomes our way, our truth and our life.

In conclusion we can say that our spiritual life is a journey. It is a journey from God outside to God inside, from the Law to the Kingdom of God, from Moses to Christ, from the Old (first) Covenant to the New Covenant, from external Temple to inner Temple, from external (old) Jerusalem to inner (new) Jerusalem. It is a journey of repentance or conversion. It is going through the narrow gate. It is the journey of inner transformation. In this journey, we begin with Moses, representing the Law, and pass through John the Baptist and Virgin Mary and arrive at Christ, the kingdom of God. It is the final destiny of our spiritual evolution or journey. Christ invited his disciples to grow into this kingdom and he gave them the mission to help others to do the same.

6.
A dance of transformation

The process of unfolding

Before time began there was only one Reality. It was fullness of Being, fullness of Consciousness and fullness of Joy. It was Unity and Love. Unity was dancing in sheer joy pouring out its true nature.

Unity said to itself: let us share our joy. Let us unfold a being in our own image and likeness. It will be dependent on us and can experience our joy. It will not be outside of us as nothing can exist outside of us. So Unity unfolded a being: universal consciousness. The Word that contained all the words and all the worlds. It is only one and there is nothing else. Unity could see its reflection in it.

Unity said to the Word: you are our Beloved Manifestation. Dance with us and experience our joy. So Unity and the Word danced together: Unity in its own joy and the Word rejoicing in the joy of Unity.

Then Unity said to the Word: unfold many words so that they too may dance with us and share our joy. The Word unfolded many words and many groups of people separate from each other joined the dance. They danced with happiness in their collective groups seeing the presence of the Word only in their own group but not aware that other groups existed also. Now the Word manifested into collective words.

As time passed the individuals in the group felt oppressed by the group. They wanted to be free and live only for themselves. So they broke away from their groups and began to dance on their own. They identified the Word only with their individuality and thus fragmented the Truth into individuals, forgetting their group, other groups, the Word and Unity. Yet they danced with joy. Since they lived only for themselves they became selfish and used others for their happiness. So their dance of joy turned into a dance of individual violence.

The process of ascending

Unity became aware of this and told the Word: there is so much individual violence in the world. Individuals are living only for themselves treating others merely as their objects. It is not good for humanity. Help human beings to realize the Truth and return to unity. The Word inspired the individuals to see the truth, to see the limitations of their understanding. So as time passed the individuals realized that they were selfish and were creating individual violence in the world. They felt the need to belong to a group and live for others and not to live only for themselves. So they returned to their collective groups. Now they began to dance in groups again. It was a dance of joy. They thought only their group contained the truth. Slowly they noticed other groups also and felt them to be enemies. They began to fight with other groups and created a collective violence in the world. Their dance of joy turned into a dance of violence.

The Divine became aware of this and told the Word: there is no joy in the world but only collective violence. Each group is trying to eliminate the other group. This is not good for humanity. Help them to see the Truth.

The Word inspired the groups to see the limitations of their understanding of the Truth. So as time passed each group realized that they were fragmenting the Word into collective groups and thus causing collective violence in the world. So they felt the need for unity. All the groups returned to the Universal consciousness, into the Word. They began to dance as one group, one humankind and one creation. It was the dance of joy. Unity felt very happy. Unity said: let the Word realize its unity with us. Let it realize that it is not only our manifestation but it also has the possibility to realize its oneness with us. So Unity inspired the Word to return to itself. And the Word, the universal consciousness, returned to Unity and danced the dance of eternity. In the Word the whole of humanity and creation entered into Unity, as if the whole of creation has melted back into Unity. The Word entered into the stage before Unity manifested the creation.

The process of returning

Now Unity said: let the Word return to the manifestation with this new awareness and dance with us. So the Word came out of Unity and danced the dance of universal consciousness. Naturally the Word manifested the collective groups and people began to dance collectively. But the groups were not separated anymore. They were linked to other groups and each group formed the shape of a nest from where to grow into the universal consciousness. Each collective group realized that the purpose of all collective groups was the same. There was no more collective violence in the world and there was peace. It was the dance of joy. The Word brought forth individuals and each individual began to dance not in isolation but holding hands with others. They realized they were all interconnected and could not do anything without the others. They did not claim any of their actions as their own but as the actions of Unity. There was no more individual violence but only joy and peace. Each individual saw himself or herself as the manifestation of the Divine and they saw others also in the same way.

TRUTH IN DIALOGUE

7.
The prayer of Christopher

Christa Prema, which means love of Christ, was a great sage.

He taught that there is only one God, one eternal Reality and that one God manifested this entire universe. Human beings are part of this universe. Their vocation is to allow God to work in and through them. They are to be instruments of God. They are to manifest divine attributes of love and compassion in loving relationships. The difference between human beings and all other creatures is that human beings have the possibility to forget their vocation and live in ignorance. When they do that they live in selfishness and make God into their instrument. This selfishness will produce individual desires and collective desires and thus create individual and collective violence in the world. The primary purpose of our human existence is to remember that we are all one in that one eternal Reality and to manifest divine attributes of love and compassion in our relationships. It is to transform our life into a life of God and our actions into actions of God.

Christopher (which means bearer of Christ) was a poor boat-man in a small village. One day he went to Christa Prema and said: Teacher, my name is Christopher and I am a boat-man from the nearby village. I ferry people everyday. I receive every day around fifty passengers and I charge each passenger five rupees and earn every day around two hundred and fifty rupees which is enough to maintain my family.

76 WHAT IS TRUTH?

I wish to earn more money and live a comfortable life. Please teach me a prayer so that my wish may be fulfilled.

Christa Prema said to Christopher: my son, I will teach you a prayer. Say that prayer every day before you go to bed. Your wish will come true.

This is the prayer: O God, I thank you for the gift of my life. I thank you so much for sending fifty passengers a day so that I can earn two hundred and fifty rupees per day. This helps me to sustain my family. Please send more passengers from tomorrow so that I can earn a little more money and live comfortably.

Christopher said this prayer every night. God blessed him day after day and more passengers came to him. He earned more money and began to live a comfortable life. This continued for many years.

One day Christopher came back to Christa Prema and said: Teacher, thank you so much for the prayer you taught me. I have been saying that prayer every night and God blessed me so much that I got more passengers everyday and earned more money. Now I live a comfortable life. But these days I am not quite happy in my heart. I feel something is missing. Are working, earning money and living a comfortable life, the ultimate purpose of my life? I feel as if I am using God as an instrument to make my life comfortable. Please help me.

Christa Prema was pleased with the question of Christopher and said to him: my son God is blessing you. I will teach you another prayer.

From today onwards say this prayer: O God, I thank you for the gift of my life. I thank you so much for giving me the opportunity to ferry my neighbours. I am so happy in doing service to my neighbours. May I have this opportunity every day until the end of my life. Thank you also for giving me enough money to sustain my family.

Christopher said this prayer every night. God blessed him and gave him happiness and contentment. This went on for several years.

One day Christopher came back to Christa Prema and said: Teacher, thank you so much for the prayer you taught me. I have been saying that prayer every night. I feel contentment in my heart and I do not have longing for more money and other material things. I do not work only for money but to serve my neighbours. I rejoice in this service. But still I feel something is missing in me and I do not understand why. Is serving my neighbours the ultimate meaning and purpose of my life? Please help me.

Christa Prema was happy with the question of Christopher and said: my son, God is blessing you. I will teach you another prayer.

From today onwards say this prayer: O God, I thank you for the gift of my life. I thank you so much for giving me the opportunity to ferry 'you' many times a day. I am so happy for doing this. May I have this opportunity to serve you every day until the end of my life. Thank you for giving me enough money to sustain my family.

Christopher said this prayer every night. He saw God in every person and he was serving God in every person. He was more happy and joyful than before. This went on for several years.

One day Christopher again came back to Christa Prema and said: Teacher, thank you for the prayer you taught me. I have been saying that prayer every night. I felt so happy that I could see God in every person and I could serve God in every person. But still I find something is missing in me, something incomplete. I do not understand why. Is seeing God in the other the ultimate meaning and purpose of my life? Please help me.

Christa Prema was happy with the question of Christopher and said: my son, God is blessing you.

I will teach you a different prayer and from today onwards say this prayer: O God, I thank you for the gift of my life. I realize that you alone are. You are the foundation of my life, like the earth that supports a tree. You are the sun and I am its ray. It is you who are in me and it is you who are in the others. It is you who are ferrying yourself. So far I thought it was 'I' who was doing this work. I was in ignorance. The works which I am doing are not my own but it is you, who dwell in me, who are doing your works. Thank you for removing my ignorance and helping me to see the truth. May I live in this awareness until the end of my life; in fact my life is your life. Thank you also for giving me necessary money to sustain my family; in fact my family is your family.

Christopher said this prayer every night. He understood the ultimate meaning and purpose of his life. He was filled with the fullness of joy and happiness.

One day Christopher went back to Christa Prema and said: Teacher, thank you so much for the prayer you taught me. I am filled with the fullness of joy and happiness. I have seen the ultimate meaning and purpose of my life. I will always be grateful to you.

Christ Prema took Christopher into his hands and said: my son, may I have many disciples like you. I am very impressed by your dedication for the search of truth. May you live the truth you have realized!

May the world be full of people like Christa Prema and Christopher!

8.
Guidelines for inter-religious dialogue

All the sacred scriptures are a gift of God to humanity. They reveal God's concern and care for humanity. They reveal the will of God to humanity and also give guidance to men and women about how to live their lives in the world of time and space. All religions have their basis in the sacred scriptures. We can say that all religions are like different houses built by God according to the need of the people for whom he is building the houses. In this sense the sacred scriptures are conditioned by the social, political and scientific development of the people living in a particular time.

As human consciousness grows, the understanding of God also grows. Our journey to God is like climbing a hill. On this journey we may build temporary houses for rest until we reach the top of the hill where we experience the fullness of Truth. Different religions are like different houses built on this hill and sometimes they can be at different levels and on different sides of the hill. God allows this building of the houses as a temporary settlement. The danger comes only when they are turned into permanent settlements. They should be like tents, temporary shelters, but if they are made like concrete buildings, then people stop their journey to God and are concerned only with the building. Though these houses are built by human beings according to their needs, we can nevertheless say that they are also in the plan of God. But we cannot say that God has built the final and perfect house (religion). It does not exist. If we say that God has built a final house or revealed a final religion, then we limit God's infinity and human potential for growth and creativity.

A final religion or a final scripture is not to the benefit of humanity. All religions and scriptures are only ladders. The purpose of all scriptures and all religions is to help human beings find their union with God. From this union comes inner peace and happiness. Their purpose is to help human beings discover their deepest inner reality where God or True Self can be found.

We can say without any hesitation that there is only one way to God. It is not a religion, not a person, not a technique, not a philosophy. It is to renounce our ego or ignorant self and find our true self where God is found. The purpose of every religion, philosophy, and technique is to help human beings renounce their ego or false self and find their true self.

We can describe it in another way: it is to expand our ego from the individual identity to the unitary or divine identity. Jesus described this way through a parable: 'the kingdom of God is like a mustard seed. It is the smallest of all seeds but when it grows it becomes so big that the birds of the air will come and make their nests in it' (Mt. 13:31-32). But these scriptures and religions can also become the source of conflict and violence. Today the world is divided in the name of religions. There has been so much violence in the name of religions. Even today people are killing and being killed in the name of religions. How can we really bring peace into the world?

In order to understand the place of religions we need to understand the nature of Truth. Truth has two aspects: the eternal aspect and the historical aspect. When Moses asked God about his name, first God said that 'I am what I am,' but it was difficult for Moses to understand this eternal aspect of Truth so God revealed to him his historical aspect: 'I am the God of Abraham, Isaac and Jacob.'

The historical aspect of Truth or God is manifested in time and space and it is present in the sacred scriptures. The historical manifestation of Truth is conditioned. The eternal truth can never be limited to a historical truth. The eternal truth always transcends the historical truth. The historical truth cannot bring unity among religions or humanity. Only the eternal truth can do that. Hence there is a constant need for humanity to move from the historical truth into the eternal truth. The historical truth creates an ego and can thus become an obstacle. In order to move from the historical truth into the eternal truth, we need to see the limitations of the historical truth.

Only when we see clearly the limitations of the historical truth or religions can we open ourselves to the eternal truth. So I have formulated a few questions, which can help us to study each religion and then to come to an understanding of each religion:

1. What were the fundamental questions asked at the beginning of each religion's spiritual search? Each religion is unique because each religion is trying to answer some particular questions.

2. What is the highest divine-human relationship possible in this particular religion? There are three possibilities: dualistic, qualified non-dualistic, and non-dualistic.

3. What type of revelation do we have in this particular religion? There are three possibilities: the revelation of a Book or Law, the revelation of

the universal mind, and the revelation of the identity of human consciousness with the divine 'I AM.'

4. What is the status of men and women in this particular religion? Are they equal? Do they have equal possibilities? If they do not have equal possibilities then the religion needs reformation. It needs to grow.

5. What is the relationship between spirituality and the social realities of the world like poverty, social discrimination, and social, economic and political oppression? Is religion only personal or has it a message for the social problems?

6. What is the relationship between spirituality and ecology? What is the place of creation in spirituality? Is creation only an object for human beings to enjoy or is it a manifestation of God? Are human beings masters of creation or guardians of creation?

7. What is relationship between spirituality and sexuality? Is sex something profane or is it something sacred?

8. What is the purpose of human existence according to each religion? Do we have any positive contribution to make in this world or is this world a prison from which we need to escape as soon as possible?

These questions are not exhaustive. People can add some more if they come across other aspects to be studied in relation to religion. When we study each religion through these questions we discover that no religion is satisfactory. Each religion needs to improve itself. This realization should not discourage us. Religions are not meant to be perfect. They belong to the evolutionary process of the spiritual growth of human beings. Hence they always need to grow, to reform.

The present generation is not born just to give continuity to the historical truth but to use the historical truth in order to move into the eternal Truth. The present generation has something to contribute to this evolution.

Historical truth cannot unite humanity; only Eternal Truth can. Historical truth is like a nest where we are born, where we are protected, nourished and given security until the wings are grown that allow us to fly into the freedom of the infinite space. Eternal truth can never be codified into laws or religious beliefs and structures. The difficulty comes when we transform the nest into a cage and imprison ourselves in the cage of historical truth.

The best way of having inter-religious dialogue is for each religion to present its unique manifestation or revelation of truth—but also for each religion to have the courage and humility to present its limitations or areas which need to be improved. Only then we can have fruitful inter-religious dialogue.

9.
Diversity, uniqueness and unity

'Blessed are the pure in heart for they shall see God,'[54] said Jesus.

Purity of heart and mind is an essential condition for those who are on the path of Truth. We all believe that there can be only one God or one Source. We all come from that one Source and we all return to that one Source. All the great sages or masters drink from the same Source and bring water from the same Source. They all speak from that same Foundation. Different religions give different names to it and each describes it in a unique way. Each great sage has a unique understanding of that Source and a unique expression of that Source. It might seem that they are not only different from each other but irreconcilable in their differences. So far religions have regularly lived apart, each one enclosed in its own boundary, often trying to expand into other boundaries, thereby becoming a source of conflict and violence. Today, thanks to God, we are in a world of inter-religious dialogue where serious efforts are being made to reconcile religions. Though these efforts have not yet produced many concrete results, it is an admirable call.

Today it is common to divide religious traditions into two main categories: the Wisdom Tradition and the Prophetic Tradition. Religions like Hinduism, Buddhism, Jainism and Daoism belong to the Wisdom Tradition and religions like Judaism, Zoroastrianism,

Christianity, Islam, and Baha'i belong to the Prophetic Tradition. Each tradition has its unique approach to the Truth. This division helps us to understand the uniqueness of each spiritual tradition and also the differences between them.

The future of humanity depends on the marriage of these two traditions.

In this article I will attempt to show the common spiritual journey in three of these religions: Hinduism, Buddhism and Christianity. I want to show that, (1) the starting conditions of each of these spiritual traditions are different, (2) each of these spiritual traditions had a unique experience of that Source, and (3) at the Source of each of these three spiritual traditions there is an essential unity. I am not trying to present an elaborate scientific explanation but rather an intuitive, synthetic presentation that will allow us to see common elements in the three religions.

The Upanishad Sages and Hinduism

I will first take the teaching of the Mandukya Upanishad and the Chandogya Upanishad of Hinduism in order to discern a common thread in the above-mentioned three religions. (Each Upanishad has a unique approach to the Truth even though the essential Truth of all Upanishads is the same: the identity of Atman with Brahman).

These two Upanishads present the nature of truth or reality according to four levels of consciousness. The first level is called 'waking consciousness,' the second level is called 'dreaming consciousness,' the third is 'deep-sleep consciousness,' and the fourth 'awakened consciousness.' The first three levels have both physical and spiritual aspects.

1. Waking consciousness, physically speaking, means to be in a state of physical wakefulness. It is the state of consciousness from the time we get up in the morning to the time we go to sleep. Here our senses are awake. As a way of living, waking consciousness means a state of life in which we identify with our physical body and live to satisfy only our physical desires and ambitions. Everything that we do is intended to satisfy the needs of our body and the senses. We can say that in waking consciousness our senses are awake and indulge in their satisfaction. Here our identity is with the body: I am my body. We can describe this level as 'individual mind' or 'individual consciousness.' Here truth is individualistic. A person says: I (body, the individual) am the way, the truth and the life. It is a very materialistic view.

2. Dreaming consciousness, understood physically, means the time when we enter into a state of dreaming while physically asleep; it lasts up to the time when the dreams come to an end. Understood spiritually, it means living our life according to dreams or ideals. In this consciousness we have ideals to follow and ideal persons to imitate. In general, these ideals and ideal persons are taken from the past. We are inspired by the great personalities and their ideals and wish to imitate them. We place our body and senses under the guidance of these ideals and ideal persons. Here the past enters into the present and goes to the future. The present is just a vehicle for the past to go to the future. The present does not have its own life but allows the past to live in and through it. Here the present is at the service of the past even though some changes can be made now and then, by way of reformation. The present is not free. The present receives its identity from the past. All religious ideals belong to dreaming consciousness.

Here our identity leads each of us to affirm: 'I am a Hindu,' or 'I am a Buddhist,' or 'I am a Jew,' or 'I am a Christian,' etc. We can call this consciousness 'collective mind' or 'collective consciousness.' This collective consciousness unites us with some persons and divides us from others. This consciousness has a boundary to protect and also a possible mission to expand. Here a person's life is guided by the moral code of a particular religion. Here truth is an ideal, a belief structure. A person will say: my religion or ideal is the way, the truth and the life.

3. Deep-sleep consciousness, physically speaking, means a dreamless sleep state. It is a state from the time when dreams stop to the time when they begin again. Spiritually, it means a state in which the dreams come to an end–dreams in the sense of ideals and ideal persons. It means the past comes to an end. When the past comes to an end the future also comes to an end, for the future is nothing but the continuity of the past. In this freedom from the past and the future, the present becomes original and creative. It connects itself to the eternal Reality (God) and manifests eternity in the present. Here one's identity is not with the body or with one's ideals but with eternity. A person will say: 'I am' (though not in the sense of the divine I AM). We can call this level 'universal mind' or 'universal consciousness.' Here a person identifies with all and lives for all. In this consciousness there are no ideological boundaries. This 'I am' transcends all the boundaries. It has no boundary to protect and so no mission to expand. It invites people to transcend collective consciousness and enter into universal consciousness. It is an all-embracing consciousness. In this consciousness a person is not guided by an external moral code but by inner realization. Here truth is universal. A person will say: I am the way, the truth and the life. Whatever this person does to others, he or she does to himself or herself.

4. Awakened Consciousness is a consciousness where a person realizes being one with Brahman or Atman or God. A person declares, 'I am Brahman' (aham Brahma asmi). We can call this level 'unitary consciousness' or 'non-dual consciousness' (Advaita). Here one's identity is 'I AM' (the 'I AM WHO I AM' of the Bible). Here truth is God. A person will say: Brahman or God is the way, the truth and the life. This I AM is Real and eternal, while the other three levels of consciousness are described as unreal or non-eternal. Real is that which has no beginning and end and Unreal is that which has beginning and end. Since Brahman, the awakened consciousness, has no beginning and end it is called Real (Sat, eternal); and the other three levels do have beginning and end so they are called unreal. Our spiritual journey is to go from the unreal to the Real. We have the famous prayer in the Upanishads that says:

> Lead me from the unreal to the Real,
> From darkness to Light,
> From death to Eternal Life.

According to the Mandukya and Chandogya Upanishads, a person begins his/her understanding with the first level of consciousness and then slowly moves into the fourth level of consciousness. It is a long journey. In the Chandogya Upanishad, Prajapathi, the spiritual teacher or guru, guides his disciple, Indra, to realize this truth. For Indra it takes a total of 101 years. The first stage lasts 32 years, the second stage 32 years, the third stage 32 years, and the fourth 5 years. These are symbolic numbers to show that the journey is long and hard. One needs to have strong determination, dedication, self-enquiry, and devotion to the master and to the truth. One should not settle down on the way like the disciple Virochana, who was satisfied with the first stage, nor should one be content simply with the sacred scriptures, which belong to the second level, for a person who moves into universal consciousness is greater than the scriptures.

The Mundaka Upanishad speaks of two types of wisdom: Para Vidhya (higher wisdom or non-dualistic experience, advaita) and Apara Vidhya (lower wisdom or dualistic experience). Para Vidhya is the direct experience of Truth and Apara Vidhya is indirect understanding of it. Even the four Vedas (revealed truth) belong to the lower wisdom. We begin with Apara Vidhya and move into Para Vidhya.

The Upanishad sages were universal spirits and so cannot be put into any category like Hinduism. Hinduism is a system of beliefs, whereas the sages were beyond beliefs.

The Buddha and Buddhism

I will now take the four levels of consciousness of the Upanishads and use them to interpret the spiritual journey of the Buddha and the different bodies of the Buddha in Buddhism.

Hinduism and Buddhism can be referred to as sister religions. There are some concepts–like Karma, Reincarnation, Dharma, and Sannyasa–which are common to both. The Buddha rejected the over-intellectualism of the Upanishads, the violent animal sacrifices of Vedic rituals, and the social caste system which gave a dominant place to the Brahmin caste. He opened the possibility of spiritual life to everyone, including women. He rejected the authority of the Vedas and rejected the division of life into four stages of Brahmacharya (spiritual student life), grhasta (family life), vanaprasta (eremitical life), and Sannyasa (wandering life). We can say that he rejected varnasramadharma which is the foundation of Hinduism. While in Hinduism only Brahmins had the possibility to adopt a life of renunciation after fulfilling their family responsibilities, Buddha offered this possibility to all castes whenever they wished. It represented a tremendous liberation to the lower castes to think that they too could take up a life of renunciation. Buddha even offered this possibility to women (even though he placed them beneath men) which was not a possibility in Hinduism. In this sense, Buddha was a revolutionary.

But there are also many similarities between Buddhism and Hinduism, some of which become clear if we look at four important stages in the life of the Buddha.

1. *Siddhartha, the man:*
   The Buddha began his life as Siddhartha, the son of a local king near the border of present-day India and Nepal. Siddhartha was the individual consciousness of the Buddha, his waking consciousness. He tried to find fulfilment in his physical desires and ambitions but was not satisfied. He felt something was missing, so he left his wife, his son, his parents, and his kingdom and went off in search of freedom.

2. *Siddhartha, the seeker:*
   After leaving his wife, child, and home, Siddhartha became a seeker. He tried to follow the different types of spiritual path that existed at that time in order to find what he was looking for: inner freedom and peace. We can say that he was living in dreaming consciousness, pursuing ideals and ideal persons. He was not yet original but was simply imitating others. But he was not satisfied with the teachings that he received and he set out on his own spiritual practices. He became disillusioned with these practices, which brought him even to the brink of physical death.

3. *Siddhartha becomes a Buddha, an Awakened One:*
   Disappointed with his practices, Siddhartha sat under the Bodhi tree in deep meditation, which opened him to the universal mind or consciousness. He moved beyond the past and the future into eternity and tasted timeless reality. From that eternity he saw the passing moments of time, which are the product of desire. He became awakened, the Buddha, and achieved freedom, nirvana. This universal consciousness existed before Siddhartha. Buddhism teaches that Siddhartha was not the first one to realize this truth—before him many others had realized it. Siddhartha is one of the Buddhas and not the only one. At this level he entered into deep-sleep consciousness and became an original person who proposed his own original way to the Truth instead of repeating someone else's discovery or truth. He became an original teacher and spoke from his own inner authority.

4. *Siddhartha the Buddha established in Buddha-nature:*
   Siddhartha was not only awakened (the Buddha) but was also established permanently in that awakened consciousness. He was ever wakeful, in a permanent state of unity. This experience of the Buddha we can call 'unitary consciousness,' 'non-dual consciousness,' or advaita.

In sum, we have Siddhartha the man (individual consciousness), Siddhartha the pursuer of ideals (collective consciousness), Siddhartha, a Buddha (awakened, deep-sleep consciousness), and Siddhartha the Buddha permanently established in wisdom (unitary consciousness).

These four stages could also be expressed using terms that are explicitly Buddhist. That tradition speaks of three bodies (Kayas) of the Buddha: the Nirmana Kaya (physical), the Samboghya Kaya (universal), and the Dhamma Kaya or Dharma Kaya (the Ground), but we could add one more body, the body of his teachings, and call it dhamma kaya (with a lower-case 'd'). Hence the Buddha can be said to have four bodies or four levels of consciousness.

1. *Nirmana Kaya*
   is the physical body of the Buddha, Siddhartha. But after his enlightenment his body extends also to the whole physical universe, for the whole universe or manifested world is the physical body of the Buddha.

2. *Dhamma Kaya*
   is the teachings of Buddha. These are the spoken words of the Buddha as recorded in history. They became a source of authority for Buddhism.

3. *Samboghya Kaya*
   is the universal body of the Buddha, beyond time and space. It is the universal consciousness of the Buddha, the bridge between Dhamma Kaya on the one hand and dhamma Kaya and Nirmana Kaya on the other. Samboghya Kaya is not limited by the teachings of dhamma Kaya. Rather, it is the Word from which all the words or teachings come. This Word cannot be put into words. The Word is like infinite space, whereas the words (teachings) are like the space between four walls.

4. *Dhamma Kaya*
   is the eternal aspect of Buddha. It is greater than Samboghya Kaya and is like the hub of a wheel. It is the foundation of all the bodies, holding all the other bodies and transcending them. We can call this 'unitary consciousness' or 'non-dualistic consciousness.'

If we take the symbol of a tree, the leaves would represent Nirmana Kaya, the branches would represent dhamma Kaya, the trunk Samboghya Kaya, and the roots Dhamma Kaya. There is only one tree, but it manifests on four levels.

From this perspective, dhamma Kaya (the branches) is greater than Nirmana Kaya (Siddhartha, the leaf) in that it lives longer than physical Siddhartha. Samboghya Kaya (the trunk) is greater than dhamma Kaya as it supports the teachings (branches) but is not conditioned by them; Samboghya Kaya can modify the expressions of dhamma Kaya. Dhamma Kaya (the roots) is greater than Samboghya Kaya as Samboghya Kaya is manifested body and Dhamma Kaya is unmanifested body. Dhamma Kaya stands by itself. It is like Brahman of Vedas. It is eternal. Hence the Buddha cannot be limited to his physical body and to his teachings. He is not confined to his teachings but is greater than them and even has power to change them. The primary mission of the Buddha was to invite people to grow into Dhamma Kaya and not just to establish dhamma Kaya (a body of teachings). The body of his teachings is like a raft that one uses to cross the river of samsara into nirvana. It is the bridge between samsara and nirvana. Samsara is the state of ignorance in which a person is driven by his/her desires and Nirvana is freedom from desires. A person lives from inner freedom.

Christ and Christianity

Retaining our emphasis on the number four, we can also see four important stages in the spiritual journey of Jesus:

1. *Jesus, the Man:*
   The first stage of Jesus was his physical birth and physical identity. He was a man. As a physical body, he had an individual consciousness of his own. This was his waking consciousness.

2. *Jesus, the Jew:*
   After his circumcision Jesus became part of Jewish collective consciousness. He was not only a man physically but also a Jew. As a Jew he was united with all other Jews but separated from non-Jews, the so-called Gentiles. As a Jew he had the Law, the Torah, as his ideal and great personalities of his tradition like Abraham, Isaac, Jacob and Moses as models whom he might imitate. The Jewish belief structure was his dreaming consciousness. At this stage Jesus was not original, for he still belonged to his spiritual tradition and gave continuity to it, being guided by its moral code. As a Jew he might have said: Judaism is my way, my truth and my life. But he began to realize the limitations of his religion—he was not satisfied. This brought him to the third important moment of his life, his baptism.

3. *Jesus the Christ, the Son of God:*
   At the moment of his baptism Jesus moved away from the collective consciousness of Judaism and entered into the 'universal mind' or 'universal consciousness.' He realized himself as the Son of God and experienced the New Covenant, the Law within or Truth within. Here his identity was just 'I am,' which was freedom from the past and the future. He went beyond the Torah and could say: 'it is written in your Law, but I say unto you'. He became free and original. He proposed his own way to the Truth, becoming an authority based on his own experience. We can say that at the moment of his baptism Jesus came out of his dreaming consciousness (Judaism) and entered into 'deep-sleep consciousness.' Here he could say: 'I am the way, the

truth and the life'. As the Son of God, he is the bridge between God and the people. He is like a trunk.

4. *Jesus Christ one with God:*
    Jesus moved one step higher and realized himself as being one with God: 'the Father and I are one', he declared. He established himself in that eternal oneness with God. This was his fourth level of consciousness. Here, God is the way, the truth and the life. Jesus said: 'the works which I do are not my own but the Father who dwells in me does his works'.

In this sense we can also say that Jesus has four bodies. The first one is Jesus of Nazareth, the physical body (Nirmana Kaya or waking consciousness). It appeared two thousand years ago and ended after the thirty-three years of his earthly life. The second body is his teachings (dhamma Kaya or dreaming consciousness), which are two thousand years old and continue to guide a large section of humanity today. The third is his universal body (Samboghya Kaya, the Universal or cosmic Christ), which is not confined to time and space but is present everywhere. This universal body existed before his physical body and teachings. The final body, the fourth, is his unity with the Father, God (Brahman and Dhamma Kaya). As Saint John says: 'in the beginning was the Word, the Word was with God and the Word was God... The Word became flesh and dwelt among the people.' God manifested everything in and through that Word. Jesus' teachings are higher than his physical body as they last longer than his physical body. His universal body (Word) is higher than his teachings, for we cannot reduce the Word into his words or his teachings.

The Son of God or universal body is not identical with his teachings. He can even change his teachings according to the situation in which he gives them. His divine oneness is higher than his universal body because the universal body still belongs to the level of manifestation. The Word was God. His divine oneness is the foundation of the other three levels just like the hub from which the spokes of a wheel radiate. Jesus came from God and returned to God. In Christianity we say that Jesus is one hundred per cent divine and one hundred per cent human. He is a hundred percent human on the lower three levels and is a hundred percent divine on the fourth level.

This could also be said of the Upanishad sages and the Buddha. The Upanishad sages were a hundred per cent divine on the fourth level of consciousness, from which they were able to say, aham Brahma asmi ('I am Brahman'). But they were also a hundred percent human on the lower three levels. The same applies to the Buddha: he was a hundred per cent divine in his Dhamma Kaya and a hundred per cent human in the lower three bodies.

Individual Sages and Universal Mind

We need to distinguish between the individual sages of the Upanishads and the universal mind. The individual sages, as physical bodies, are not identical with universal consciousness, for the latter was there before the individual sages. It manifests through them but it does not exhaust itself in them. It is for this reason that the same truth is communicated through each sage in a unique way. Each Upanishad explains the same truth in its unique way. No sage has the last word on it. Interestingly the Hindu tradition does not give much importance to the physical bodies of these sages; there is not much worship and veneration of them. The emphasis is on their teachings and on the eternal Brahman and Atman.

Siddhartha and the Buddha

We also need to make a distinction between Siddhartha and the Buddha, for they are not identical. Buddha consciousness is before Siddhartha. The Buddha manifested in Siddhartha but is not exhausted in Siddhartha. Siddhartha entered into the consciousness of the Buddha, but the Buddha is greater than Siddhartha. There were many persons who were awakened to Buddha consciousness before Siddhartha was. Siddhartha was not the only Buddha but one of many. Even though in Buddhism the emphasis is on finding Nirvana, there is also much veneration of the physical form of the Buddha, Siddhartha.

Jesus and the Christ

The same principle applies to Jesus also. We need to make a subtle distinction between Jesus and the Christ. Jesus, as a physical body, is not identical with the Christ, the universal consciousness. Christ consciousness was there before Jesus. Christ consciousness manifested in Jesus but it does not exhaust itself in Jesus. Jesus, as a physical body, had a beginning and an end, but the Christ, as the universal consciousness, has no beginning or end. Jesus, as a body, is one leaf on the tree, whereas the Christ is the trunk. The consciousness of the leaf has entered into the consciousness of the trunk but is not identical with it. There are also many other leaves on the trunk. However, it seems that in Judaism this experience has no precedent. No one in that tradition had this experience before Jesus. He was the first one to claim this experience and for that reason came into conflict with the spiritual authorities of his tradition and was accused of blasphemy.

Diversity, Uniqueness and Unity

On the first level of consciousness, which is the physical level, the Upanishad Sages, Siddhartha, and Jesus are different. They are born in different times and different socio-political and spiritual conditions. It seems that the search of the Upanishad sages began during the period when belief in the efficacy of Vedic rituals was declining and there was enough economic prosperity for people to have the time and leisure to ask fundamental questions of life. They focused on the eternal, the Real. The answer they found was Atman and Brahman. They kept their discovery as a secret and communicated it only to those who they thought were worthy of it. They were not missionaries.

We know that Siddhartha was born into a royal family about 500 years before Jesus. He had his own personal questions. He was not happy with the Vedic sacrifices and was dissatisfied with the extreme intellectualism of the Vedic sages. He was perturbed by the caste system and the division of life into different stages. He renounced his wife, his son, and his kingdom and went in search of freedom. After his enlightenment he became an itinerant missionary who dedicated his life to help sentient beings to find freedom from samsara. He died at an advanced age.

Jesus was born in Palestine at a time of Roman occupation and his people were looking for a messiah who would liberate them from Roman oppression. His society was divided into the righteous and the unrighteous. The scribes and the Pharisees considered themselves as righteous and the tax-collectors, prostitutes and sinners, those who did not keep the Law, as unrighteous. There was also the division of rich and poor. After Jesus' enlightenment he began to preach his message of the kingdom of God. His teaching became controversial. He was accused of blasphemy and met a violent death in the prime of his life.

Before his death he entrusted his mission to his disciples, who propagated his message.

On the first level of consciousness the Upanishad sages, Siddhartha, and Jesus were different. They were born in different times and different social structures and political conditions.

On the second level of consciousness also they were different. Their questions were different and their problems were different. Their philosophical and theological traditions were different. The Upanishad sages were preoccupied with the Eternal–their question was: 'what is that by finding which we find everything, and what is that by knowing which we know everything?' The answer they found was Brahman and Atman. Buddha's question was: 'what is the source of suffering and how to be free from suffering?' The answer he found was freedom from Desire. Jesus' question might have been: 'how can one establish a just society where there will be love, freedom, and equality?' The answer he found was the kingdom of God, the radical love of God and the radical love of neighbour.

On the third level of consciousness, which is universal consciousness, the Upanishad sages, the Buddha, and the Christ had the unique experience of eternal reality. The way they experienced it, described it and manifested it was unique. The way we encounter universal consciousness depends on the questions with which we make our journey. The Upanishad sages, the Buddha and Jesus Christ were unique because their questions were unique. The answer we find depends on the questions with which we begin our journey. If our questions change the answers also will change.

On the fourth level of consciousness they were all one. There is perfect unity. On the fourth level of consciousness, which is that of unitary consciousness, the Upanishad Sages, the Buddha, and the Christ are all essentially one. There is no essential difference. The unity at the fourth level is not based on concepts, which are artificial and which will be gone once a person changes his concepts. There the unity is essential. They began differently, they experienced uniquely but they realized unity.

Inter-religious Dialogue

In inter-religious dialogue our focus is on the teaching body of the Upanishad sages, Buddha, and Christ. This belongs to the second level of consciousness. It is not possible to arrive at a consensus at that level. We tend to imprison the sages, Buddha, and Christ in their teachings. We are looking at the trunk and the roots with the eyes of a leaf and a branch. We need to have a radical change, a *metanoia*, in our perspective. We need to move away from their teaching body into their universal body and unitary body. We need to look at the leaf, at the branch, and at the trunk from the perspective of the roots, for only then will we see the uniqueness of each branch and leaf and also their limitations.

This perspective helps us find creative answers to the questions that people are asking today. It means we need to liberate the Upanishad sages from their teachings, we need to liberate the Buddha from his teachings, and we need to liberate Christ from his teachings. The Upanishad sages are not identical with Hinduism, the Buddha is not identical with Buddhism, and Christ is not identical with Christianity. Universal Consciousness is one. It has manifested itself in a unique way in the Upanishad sages, it has manifested itself in a unique way in Siddhartha, and it has manifested itself in a unique way in Jesus but it does not exhaust itself in them. This consciousness was there before them and it will continue to be so in the future. It will manifest itself in a unique way for our times, provided that we make our journey with our own specific, unique and original questions. Our original and creative questions bring original and creative answers from God.

If we begin our search with someone's questions, the answers we get will be his or hers. It would be a mechanical process. We need to ask original questions according to the situations we find ourselves in. That is what the Upanishad sages, Siddhartha, and Jesus did. For this we need to have a pure mind and a pure heart that are willing to free themselves from their conditionings and become a virgin giving birth to the original and creative truth.

'Blessed are the pure of heart for they shall see God [Truth]'.

10.
Beyond theism and atheism

There are heated arguments going on between theism and atheism. Recently when the famous scientist Stephen Hawkins made a statement that God is not necessary to explain the origin of the universe, the atheists were jubilant having found a strong ally in a theoretical physicist—whereas the religious leaders reacted negatively.

Atheists have become as missionary-like as theists in propagating their atheism. Atheistic secularism is spreading very fast and religious people are trying to confront it. There seems to be a real conflict between theism and atheism. Can we find a creative solution out of this conflict?

It is the contention of the author that theism should not look upon atheism as its enemy but as something that belongs to the evolutionary process of human consciousness towards its ultimate destiny. Theism should use the insights of atheism as a catalyst for its own evolution. Atheism should involve in a constructive and responsible critique of theism keeping in mind that its conclusions may imply that the people who believed in God in the past were in God delusion and the people who believe in God today are in God delusion.

If atheism draws its strength solely from theism's shadow-side—and solely from the conclusions of science, which by definition can only tell what things are but not why they are—then it is building its house on sand. It must open itself to Reality—Reality which is the source of all religions but which is much vaster than they. Reality which gives meaning and purpose to our human existence and which gives inner freedom. What both theism and atheism need is humility to learn and to grow. This attitude forces us to reflect on the nature of Truth.

Truth and Religious Absolutism

Religious Absolutism is that in which each religion claims to have the absolute truth. Its followers believe that their scripture has been revealed by God and that it is eternal. Followers are asked to submit their will and intellect to the authority of the sacred scripture and to the religious authorities who have the sole authority of interpreting the scripture. Religious absolutism distrusts the power of reason alone to arrive at the truth; it insists on belief or faith in the supernatural. It also enjoins its followers to be loyal, to defend its faith and propagate it, even if it involves giving one's life for it.

Religious Absolutism has a positive role to play. It gives meaning, purpose, direction, a sense of identity and security to one's life. One does not need to think too much because everything is being told. One has plenty of time to do other things instead of searching for truth. Even if one does think it is only to defend one's belief structure. One needs only to believe and to follow. In life's crises people find support and consolation in their God or belief structures.

The limitations of Religious Absolutism are that it limits spiritual life only to beliefs and thus blocks the spiritual evolution of human consciousness. It does not give freedom to think, speak or act independently as everything is already decided by Scripture or by God. It does not encourage critical thinking and investigation. It also becomes a source of division, conflict and violence in the world as human beings are divided on the lines of beliefs. It creates collective consciousness and breeds religious fundamentalism.

Atheistic Secularism

Secularism demands freedom to think, to speak and to act. It is not certain about God or an after-life but is concerned with finding fulfilment in this life. It blames religions or God as being the source of violence and bloodshed in the world. It tries to demolish the power of religion. It considers religion superstitious and fanatical, an obstacle to the freedom of human beings. It wants to free human beings from the power of God or religions. It relies on the power of reason and the gift of natural sciences to achieve its goal. Though secularism began as agnostic it later became atheistic. The secularism that tries to eliminate God completely from the public life is called aggressive secularism. We find this in the effort of secularists, in Europe and America, to remove religious education from the public schools and replace it completely with secular education. God is seen as someone who oppresses human beings and his elimination is necessary if human beings want to be free. When Frederick Nietzsche in The Gay Science declared: 'God is dead', he was announcing the death of the God of history, identified with the Biblical God, and opened the possibility for the birth of a new human consciousness, which he labelled 'higher man' (uber menschen).

Basing itself on scientific investigation, secularism has a positive contribution to make for the evolution of human consciousness as it reveals the limitations of religions and belief structures. Religion without scientific knowledge becomes superstitious.

Secularism also gives human beings the freedom and responsibility to create their own destiny. Mature secularism may focus on human dignity and human values of freedom, liberation, equality and justice. It is true that imparting religious education to children creates divisive consciousness among them from a tender age and thus sows the seeds of violence and conflict.

But Secularism has its own limitations. If children are not given any moral or religious education, even though it has its limitations, then they will be left alone without any values to guide them. However noble the ideal of secular humanism or secular spirituality may be it cannot satisfy the deep longing of our human heart. As St. Augustine said, perhaps simplistically but so memorably, 'O Lord, our hearts are made for you and they are restless until they rest in you'.

Superfluous secularism tries to free people from the concept of God and the supernatural but offers no meaningful alternative except scientific materialism, consumerism and liberalism. It plunges people into emptiness and meaninglessness and encourages them to fill that emptiness from outside. Instead of giving meaning to the (material) world human beings receive meaning from it. Instead of being salt to the world they make the world be their salt. Instead of being light to the world they make the world their light. If secularism tries to demolish religious beliefs without giving any meaningful values to live by, the result can be religious fundamentalism.

God of History and God of Eternity

This brings us to raise the most important question: what is the Truth or God? In the Mundaka Upanishad of Hinduism a disciple asks the teacher, 'Master, what is that by knowing which everything is known?'

Sages reply that there are two levels of Truth: Apara Vidhya (lower wisdom) and Para Vidhya (higher wisdom). Apara Vidhya consists of four Vedas, rituals, and other sciences. The Para Vidhya is that through which one knows God directly. Any knowledge of God that comes indirectly is lower wisdom–this even includes sacred scriptures. Higher wisdom is that in which a person has the direct experience of God and realizes the universal and indwelling presence of God. God is not outside but within. A person says, 'I am in God and God is in me'. A person may grow even further and realize that God is the source of one's existence and may declare, 'God and I are one' (aham Brahma asmi). It does not mean one becomes God or there are two Gods but it only means that ultimately God alone is, and the whole of creation comes from God and returns to God as ice comes from water and returns to it. We have to begin with Apara Vidhya and grow into Para Vidhya.

When Moses asked God his name, first God answered, 'I am who I am', but it was too much for Moses to handle. So God told him, 'I am the God of Abraham, Isaac and Jacob'. Moses could recognize God as the God of his ancestors. This is a very profound revelation on the nature of God or Truth. Truth or God has two aspects: historical and eternal. In the historical truth human beings experience God as transcendent mystery. God reveals his will through commandments such as those God gave Moses on Mount Sinai. God is greater than human beings. Human beings have to submit their will and intellect. God demands absolute obedience, loyalty and exclusivity.

But this is not the ultimate divine-human relationship. God also promised that he would make a new covenant in which he would write the Law in the heart of the people. There is no need one person telling another to know God because everyone knows God. This is the experience of the indwelling and the universal presence of God. God is no longer an authority who demands the obedience of will and intellect but he is the God of freedom who places responsibility into the hands of his mature children. God becomes silent.

Jesus Christ had this transition from the God of history to the God of eternity at the moment of his baptismal experience. He could say, 'I am in the Father (God) and the Father is in me'. He went even further when he realized his Father (God) and he were one. To say 'God and I are one' may appear to some as presumptuous and blasphemous but in fact it is a most humble statement. It is the realization of one's unity with God and with everyone, it affirms that God alone is, and we all come from God and return to God. It makes a person humble. It is the realization that everyone is that Reality (tat vam asi). Jesus washed the feet of his disciples, an act of great humility. The deeper one grows into God the humbler one becomes. Jesus inaugurated the new covenant, the new relationship with God. In this new relationship all are equal. There is no master and no disciple. One goes beyond belief and unbelief, beyond theism and atheism. God becomes completely silent. One lives by the inner wisdom and light. A person will say I am the way, the truth and the life. This is the birth of a new human being, a higher human being, who is greater than all religions, all scriptures, all philosophies and all ideologies.

All the sacred scriptures are a gift of God to humanity. But they belong to the historical manifestation of truth. Since theism is based on the sacred scriptures it also belongs to the historical manifestation of God or Truth. The historical manifestation of truth is conditioned by the times in which it is revealed. It divides human beings on the lines of sacred scriptures or religions. The difficulty comes only when historical truth is understood as eternal truth. It is like saying that the space within the four walls is the infinite space. It is like keeping people in a room locked from the inside. That understanding becomes a source of division and violence in the world. Just as every house has a door to the infinite space so also every religion should have a door to the God of eternity. God, who desires the spiritual growth of human beings, in his mercy, compassion and love, placed in every scripture the keys that open the door to the God of eternity. For their own spiritual growth and for those whom they guide, it is the responsibility of spiritual guides to look for these keys. A wise spiritual guide is one who is not only well versed in the historical God (sacred scriptures) but also established in the eternal God. He knows the place of sacred scriptures and also their limitations. In this manner he or she becomes a bridge, a way, a door for the people to cross from the historical God into the eternal God. Jesus was a true spiritual master. He was the way, the bridge, the door from the God of history to the God of eternity. He takes people beyond theism and atheism.

Jesus was very angry with the spiritual leaders of his time. He said, 'alas for you lawyers who have taken away the key of knowledge! You have not gone in yourselves and have prevented others from going in who wanted to'.[55] He felt that the spiritual leaders had become an obstacle for the spiritual growth of human beings. Jesus found these keys and used them for his spiritual growth and invited others to do the same. He gave these keys to his disciples so that they also could grow and help others do the same.

A theism that confines people to the historical manifestations of God is blocking the spiritual evolution of human consciousness and thus not cooperating with the plan of God–it may even find itself acting against the will of God. Historical manifestations of God are like the womb of God. God nourishes her children in her historical womb and gives birth to them into the infinity of eternity. Spiritual guides have two roles to play. First they need to nourish people in the womb of God of history—and then, like midwives, they should facilitate the transition into the God of eternity. It is a birthing process. Mature atheism is a cry of the human heart to free itself from the womb of the God of history and authority and move into the God of freedom and eternity. It is an existential urge to be born into a new life. It is a sign of growth. It also can be looked upon as God's indirect call to theism to open its womb to facilitate this birth of humanity into the God of eternity, into the God of freedom.

The fight of atheism is against the God of history.

It is a fight against the God of history since the God of history demands the submission of the will and the intellect; he is considered to be authoritative and oppressive. One has to free oneself from the God of history in order to enter into the God of eternity. It is a necessary process. A sign of growth.

Atheism is not recent. It began with the creation of human beings. It began when Adam and Eve rebelled against the voice of God in the Garden of Eden. They wanted to be independent of God. They were the first atheists. Both theism and atheism will be there as long as human beings exist because they belong to the evolutionary process of human consciousness. But if one halts either on theism or on atheism then one stops the evolution of human consciousness. One has to go beyond them and give birth to the God of eternity.

This is the symbolism of virgin birth in Christianity. A virgin is one who discontinues the God of history and gives birth to the God of eternity. She gives birth from above not from the past. In this process we can see two aspects: the first is the freeing from the God of history (theism). The second is the opening up to the God of eternity.

Can we intuit therefore that atheism, by negating the God of history, is also unconsciously preparing human consciousness to become virgin ready to give birth to the God of eternity?

Atheism should not limit itself to negating the God of history, it should go one step further and give birth to the God of eternity. To deny the existence of God is to deny one's own divine origin, one's own divinity, one's own eternity. It is self-dethronement. It is like a piece of ice that denies the existence of water or a leaf that denies the existence of a tree or matter that denies the existence of quarks or a car that denies the existence of petrol or a reflection in a mirror which denies that which it is reflecting.

Spiritual masters tell us that human consciousness is the reflection of divine consciousness. Human consciousness cannot exist by itself. As an analogy we can say that human consciousness has four mirrors in which the divine reflects: the mirror of matter (the body); the mirror of theism or the God of history; the mirror of atheism; the mirror of universal mind or the image and likeness of God.

Symbolically the first mirror is situated below, the second one is on the right side; the third is on the left side and the fourth is above.

The reflection in the mirror of matter sees itself as nothing but matter and declares: I am my body, I am only matter. I am a product of evolution. God does not exist.

The reflection in the second mirror on the right side feels itself to be a creature, and projects God as the creator. It encounters the God of history and declares: I am a creature of God. God is greater than me. He is holy and transcendent. I have to submit my will and intellect to the divine will.

The reflection in the third mirror on the left, the mirror of atheism, declares: I alone exist. God does not exist. God is an illusion or delusion. I am free.

The reflection in the fourth mirror of universal consciousness above realizes itself being united with everyone and everything and experiences the universal and the indwelling presence of God. It is beyond time and space. It is beyond evolutionary process. It declares: God is everywhere. Everyone and everything is in God. Everyone is in me and I am in everyone. I am in God and God in me. The works which I do are not my own but God who dwells in me does his work. This reflection knows it is free from time and becoming. It discovers its inner fullness, inner silence and inner rest. It looks into its own source, the Source, God, the reflector, and declares finally: my eternal self is God, God alone is.

This is Para Vidhya, the higher wisdom which the sage in the Mandukya Upanishad revealed to his disciple and which Jesus revealed to his disciples in the Jewish tradition.

DOES GOD EXIST?

A DISCIPLE: Master, does God exist?

MASTER: My son, do you exist?

DISCIPLE: Of course, I exist.

MASTER: If you exist then God exists.

DISCIPLE: Why?

MASTER: Because the 'I' which says 'I exist' is God.

DISCIPLE: I do not understand.

MASTER: My son, remove all the labels you have imposed on that 'I'. What remains is God.

DISCIPLE: Master, be kind enough to explain to me.

The master gave him a doll which was clothed with many layers and told him to read each label on the cloth and remove one after another.

THE DISCIPLE READ THE FIRST LABEL: I am my body. The second label: I am an engineer. The third label: I am the son/daughter of Mr. & Mrs. X. Then, I am a Tamilian, I am an Indian, I am a Christian, I am a human being, I am the creation.

The disciple removed each label in turn.

With this all the clothes had been removed. There remained only a naked doll on which was written: I AM.

DISCIPLE: Master, now I can only say: 'I AM'.

MASTER: My son that 'I AM' is God.

DOES GOD EXIST?

DISCIPLE: Master, does God exist?

MASTER: My son, does love exist?

DISCIPLE: Yes, master, love exists. There is love between parents and children, between husband and wife and so on.

MASTER: My son, if love exists, God exists, because God is love. Human love is conditioned love. God is unconditioned love. When you experience unconditioned love then you know God is. When you love some one unconditionally then you know God exists.

CAN WE SEE GOD?

A DISCIPLE: Master, can we see God?

MASTER: My son, can you see electricity?

DISCIPLE: No, master, I cannot see it.

MASTER: Do you know it is there?

DISCIPLE: Yes, I know it is there.

MASTER: How do you know it is there?

DISCIPLE: When I see the light burning, I know electricity is there.

MASTER: In the same way, my son, you cannot see God. When you are connected to God, then you know that God is there. If you are not connected to God then you may think God does not exist, but God is there. It is the light in you that reveals the existence of God.

11.
THE ETERNAL SELF AND ITS GARLAND

May we all discover our eternal self!
May we all help each other to discover our eternal self!
May we all integrate the eternal with the non-eternal!
May we all unfold love and compassion in our relationships!
May we all be a blessing to each other!
Peace, peace, peace.

Sathyaprema, which means Lover of Truth, was a great sage. She was the knower of the eternal self and helped many others to become the same. She taught that there is a self in each one of us—which is timeless, unity, freedom and peace. It has no beginning and no end. It is unborn and never dies. It does not become bigger by actions, and it does not become smaller by non-actions. It is fullness and non-dual consciousness. It is absolute good beyond relative good and evil. It stands on its own and does not depend on anything else, but everything depends on it. It is infinite Being, infinite Consciousness and infinite Joy. It unfolds the whole of the manifested world. It envelops the whole of creation and is present in every manifestation as its foundation. It is by its presence that everything lives and moves, and has its being. Human beings must know their eternal self. The persons who know their eternal self will be free from the compulsions of time and from the fear of death. They will unfold love and compassion in human relationships in the world of time and space.

Chantal was an ardent seeker of Truth. She changed her name to Sathyanvesi, which means Seeker of Truth. She heard the teachings of Sathyaprema and went to her with reverence as her spiritual student. She was eighteen years old. She stayed for one year with her teacher serving her with love and dedication. Then she asked her, 'Mother, what is my eternal self?' Sathyaprema replied, 'My daughter, go to Sathyaguha, the cave of truth and open the first door and let me know what you see there. Here is the key for it. Sathyanvesi went to Sathyaguha and opened the door. The room was fitted with a big mirror and she saw her own reflection everywhere. So she went to Sathyaprema and said, 'Mother, I see my own body. Is my body my eternal self? Am I my body?' My daughter, that is your eternal self, said Sathyaprema.

Sathyanvesi left her teacher with peace in her heart. She lived for one year satisfying all her physical needs. But she was not content. Then she began to reflect: my teacher told me that my body is my eternal self. But the eternal self has no beginning and no end and it unifies. It has no birth and death. But my body has a beginning and an end. It is born and it dies. It divides me from everyone else. My body cannot be my eternal self. So Sathyanvesi went back to Sathyaprema and stayed with her for another year with love and dedication.

After a year Sathyanvesi again asked Sathyaprema, 'Mother, teach me about my eternal self'. Sathyaprema answered, 'my daughter, go to Sathyaguha and open the second door and tell me what you see there. Here is the key for it'. Sathyanvesi went to Sathyaguha and opened the second door and again she found the room fitted with a mirror. In that mirror she saw her own image surrounded with all her family members. 'I see myself with my whole family. Is my family my eternal self?' she wondered. So she went to Sathyaprema and said, 'Mother, I see myself surrounded with my whole family'. Sathyaprema said, 'my daughter that is your eternal self'. Sathyanvesi left her teacher with peace in her heart and lived and worked for her family with love and dedication for a year.

Then she began to reflect: my teacher told me that my family is my eternal self. But my family has a beginning and an end. It unites me with all my family members but divides me from everyone else. My eternal self has no beginning and no end. It unites me with everyone and everything. I am not satisfied with this understanding.

So she again went back to Sathyaprema to be her spiritual student. She lived with her for a year with love and dedication and then asked her, 'Mother, teach me about my eternal self.' Sathyaprema replied, 'my daughter, go to Sathyaguha and open the third door and tell me what you see there. Here is the key for it'. Sathyanvesi went to Sathyaguha and opened the third door. The room was fitted with a mirror and she saw herself surrounded by all her fellow countrymen and women. 'Is my country my eternal self?' thought Sathyanvesi. She came to Sathyaprema and told her, 'Mother, I see myself surrounded by all my countrymen and women'. Sathyaprema replied, 'my daughter that is your eternal self'.

Sathyanvesi went with peace in her heart and worked for her country with love and dedication for a year. Then she began to reflect. My teacher told me that my country is my eternal self. My country unites me with all my countrymen and women wherever they may be but it also divides me from those who do not belong to my country. There is a boundary which I need to protect and there is a possibility of war at any time. My country has a beginning and a possible end, whereas my eternal self has no beginning and no end and it unites me with everyone and everything. I am not satisfied with this understanding. So Sathyanvesi returned to Sathyaprema to be her spiritual student and lived with her for a year with love and dedication.

Then she asked her, 'Mother, teach me about my eternal self'. Sathyaprema told her, 'my daughter, go to Sathyaguha, and open the fourth door and tell me what you see there. Here is the key for it'. Sathyanvesi went to Sathyaguha and opened the fourth door and again she saw the whole room fitted with a mirror. She saw herself surrounded by all her religious brothers and sisters from all over the world. 'Is my religion my eternal self?' she wondered. She went to Sathyaprema, 'Mother, I saw myself surrounded by all my religious brothers and sisters from all over the world'. Sathyaprema said, 'my daughter that is your eternal self.'

So Sathyanvesi left her teacher with peace in her heart and worked for her religion with love and dedication for a year. Then she began to reflect: my teacher told me that my religion is my eternal self, but my religion has a beginning and a possible end. It unites me with all my religious brothers and sisters wherever they may be, but it divides me from all those who do not belong to my religion, even if they are close to me. It can also create conflict with those who do not belong to my religion. The eternal self does not create divisions and does not create conflict. Hence my religion cannot be my eternal self.

So she went back to Sathyaprema to be her spiritual student and lived with her for a year. After this she asked her, 'Mother, tell me about my eternal self'. The teacher replied, 'my daughter, go to Sathyaguha and open the fifth door and tell me what you see there. Here is the key for it.' Sathyanvesi went to Sathyaguha and opened the fifth door. The room was fitted with a big mirror and she saw herself surrounded by the whole of humanity. 'Is humanity my eternal self?' she thought.

She went to Sathyaprema and told her, 'Mother, I see myself surrounded by the whole of humanity. Am I the whole of humanity?' The teacher replied, 'My daughter that is your eternal self'. Sathyanvesi left her teacher with peace in her heart and spent a year working and living for the welfare of the whole of humanity.

Then she began to reflect: I work for the whole of humanity. I am humanity. But humanity has a beginning and an end. It unites me with all human beings but divides me from non-humans. This cannot be my eternal self because my eternal self has no beginning and no end and it unites me with everyone and everything. This identity does not satisfy me.

Thinking thus, Sathyanvesi went to Sathyaprema to be her spiritual student and lived with her for another year with love and dedication. After a year she asked her teacher, 'Mother, teach me about my eternal self'. Sathyaprema replied, 'my daughter, go to Sathyaguha and open the sixth door and tell me what you see there. Here is the key for it'. Sathyanvesi went to Sathyaguha and opened the sixth door and again she found the room fitted with a big mirror. She saw herself united with the whole of creation. 'I am the whole of creation', she exclaimed. Is the whole of creation my eternal self? she wondered. She went to Sathyaprema, 'Mother, I see myself united with the whole of creation. I am the whole of creation'. 'My daughter that is your eternal self', said Sathyaprema. Sathyanvesi left her teacher with peace in her heart and lived her life united with the whole of creation. She treated all creatures, both animate and inanimate with respect and love. This she did for a year.

Then she began to reflect: My teacher told me that the whole of creation is my eternal self. But the creation has a beginning and an end.

It unites me with the whole of creation but it divides me from God. So the whole of creation cannot be my eternal self.

So she went to Sathyaprema to be her spiritual student and lived with her for another year with love and dedication. After that she asked her teacher, 'Mother, teach me about my eternal self'. Sathyaprema told her, 'my daughter, go to Sathyaguha and open the seventh door and tell me what you see there. Here is the key for it.' Sathyanvesi opened the door and expected to find a room fitted with a mirror. But to her surprise there was no room. She found herself under the infinite sky, which has no beginning and no end. Everything and everyone were contained within that infinite sky. Everything appeared to be without substance, without any substantial reality, as if it was unreal. She could see only unity. In amazement she shouted 'I AM THAT'. She felt as if she had been completely stripped and was herself standing naked under the infinite sky. Sathyanvesi was filled with joy and ran to her teacher Sathyaprema, and said, 'Mother, I see the infinite sky that contains all things. I can only say 'I AM'. I have no beginning and no end. In me everything is united. I am timeless, unity, freedom, peace. I am infinite Being, infinite Consciousness and infinite Joy'. Sathyaprema replied, 'My daughter that is your eternal self'.

Sathyanvesi left her teacher with infinite thanks and immense gratitude. She renounced the world and lived the life of a recluse. She lived in this way for a whole year. Then Sathyanvesi reflected: I Am is my eternal self, but I also have a body, a family, a nation, a religion, a humanity and creation. I know they are not my eternal self since they have a beginning and an end, yet they are there. What is the relationship between my eternal self and my non-eternal self, between the infinite and the finite?

With this question she went back to Sathyaprema, her teacher, and lived with her for another year. And then she asked her, 'Mother, I see clearly what my eternal self is and what my eternal self is not. But I wish to know what the relationship between these two is. Do I need to hold on to eternal and discard the non-eternal? Does my non-eternal self have no purpose?'

Sathyaprema replied, 'My daughter, go to Sathyaguha and enter it from the seventh door and then move backwards until you reach the first room, and then tell me what you see there. Here is the key. It can open all the doors'.

Sathyanvesi opened the seventh door from the outside and entered into the sixth room which was fitted with the mirror. She saw the whole of creation as a garland around her neck. She entered the fifth room and saw the whole of humanity as a garland around her neck. She entered the fourth room and found her religion as a garland around her neck. She entered the third room and saw her whole nation as a garland around her neck. She entered the second room and saw her entire family as a garland around her neck. Finally she entered the first room and saw her body as a garland around her neck.

When Sathyanvesi left Sathyaguha, she saw a little girl lying on the ground unconscious. Sathyanvesi ran to her and took her into her arms and placed her under a tree. Then she went and brought some water and fruits. She sprinkled water on the face of the little girl and the girl regained consciousness. She gave her some fruits to eat. As the girl ate the fruits her eyes were filled with tears of gratitude. As she finished eating, the girl smiled at Sathyanvesi and disappeared. Sathyanvesi was astonished–then she understood.

She was filled with joy and ran to her teacher and said, 'Mother, I see the non-eternal as the garland of the eternal. The eternal is the foundation and the non-eternal is its manifestation. It is the ornament of the eternal. It is its vehicle. It is the door through which the eternal self manifests its divine attributes. It is not necessary to discard it or renounce it but 'I AM' needs to wear it. 'I AM' needs it in order to make possible its flow of eternal love towards those who are in need. 'I AM' is my eternal self and the non-eternal is its body.

Sathyaprema, her teacher, was overwhelmed with joy and said, 'my daughter, you have seen the Truth. Truth is the unity of eternal and the non-eternal. It is living in relationships where we manifest or unfold divine attributes of love and compassion. I admire your love and dedication for truth. It has been a joyful time to be your teacher. May I find another student like you! Go, my daughter, go in peace.'

Sathyanvesi fell at the feet of her teacher to receive her blessings. Sathyaprema raised up her student and placed her hands on her head and blessed her: 'my daughter, may you be firmly established in your realization! May you become a bridge through which people can pass from the non-eternal to the eternal and from the eternal to the non-eternal. May you be a blessing to everyone who meets you! From now on your name will not be Sathyanvesi but you too will be called Sathyaprema for you have seen the truth. Everyone who sees the truth becomes the truth.'

Chantal became Sathyanvesi and Sathyanvesi became Sathyaprema. After that, Sathyaprema became a great sage and helped many others to become the same. May the world be filled with many people like Sathyaprema and Chantal.

12.
One Way–Many Paths
The Inclusive Way of Christ

Two of Jesus' statements are the foundational to Christianity and yet, simultaneously, problematic to inter-religious dialogue:

'I am the way, the truth and the life; no one comes to the Father except through me[56].'

and,

'Go into the whole world and proclaim the good news to the whole creation. He who believes in me will be saved and he who does not believe in me will be condemned[57].'

The first statement has been interpreted to mean that Jesus Christ is the only way to God and everyone has to believe in him in order to be saved. The second statement is interpreted to mean that Christ has given his disciples the mission to proclaim the good news to the whole creation; the good news being that Jesus Christ is the only way, the truth and the life–he is the only son of God and he is one with God. It is also seen as an invitation to non-Christians to accept this truth and convert to Christ and become Christians.

This kind of interpretation causes much conflict with other religions and obstructs inter-religious dialogue. If one holds to this outlook real dialogue becomes impossible. Other religions would like Christians to say that each religion is an equally valid way to God.

Christ is a Way to God

Christ is *a* way to God but not the only way. Official Christian churches have difficulties to accept this position. Catholics would like to say that there are seeds of truth in other religions but Christ is the fullness of truth. There is a ray of light in the other religions but Christ is the fullness of light. Their arguments have no rational basis but are based on belief. With this kind of attitude inter-religious dialogue and pluralism become a problem to the Christian believer.

Some prefer to say that 'my religion is true for me but I respect other religions'. Gandhi seems to have thought that all religions are imperfect and they need to learn from each other. Hinduism seems to be much more open to religious pluralism. There are two important statements in Hindu scriptures which reveal this openness. The first is the much-quoted statement from the Rig Veda: ekam sat vipra bahuthi vadanti, Truth (God) is one but sages describe it by many names. The second is from the Bhagavat Gita, in which Sri Krishna says to Arjuna, 'in whichever way people worship me, in the same manner I fulfil their desires (accept and bless them). O Arjuna, people follow my path in every way'.[58] The first statement gives possibility to the pluralistic expressions of God and the second statement gives possibility to the pluralistic ways to God.

Is it possible that a person like Jesus Christ who had such a profound experience of God can make statements which are so exclusive? Some think that he never made these statements. These statements are seen as expressions of the belief of the early Christian community. It is the contention of the author that Jesus certainly would have made these statements as they have universal, inclusive and liberating value. If they look exclusive it is our interpretation that needs to be questioned and not the statements themselves. The urgent need of Christianity today is to reinterpret these two statements of Jesus in such a way that they become universally valid, unifying, liberating and that they leave room for spiritual growth.

The Good News of Jesus

Jesus began his ministry proclaiming the good news of the kingdom of God saying 'the time is fulfilled; the kingdom of God is at hand; repent and believe in the good news[59].' In the gospel of Matthew we have a short version: 'repent, for the kingdom of heaven is at hand[60].'

There are many interpretations given to the expression 'kingdom of God'. The expression 'the kingdom of God' used by Jesus is packed with so many aspects that it is impossible to define. It can only be described. Jesus himself did not define it but described it in so many ways. In general, it has two aspects: objective and subjective. Objectively it reveals the universal presence of God. It means that God is everywhere and the whole of creation and humanity are within God. The statement that 'the kingdom of God is at hand' means that God is everywhere and everything and everyone is in God. The word 'repent' is an invitation to realize this truth. Subjectively it reveals the ultimate relationship of human beings with God. Human beings are ultimately one with God. Jesus said, 'the Father and I are one' (Jn.10.30). Kingdom of God is also an experience of the unconditional love of God, who radiates his love like the sun, both on the righteous and un-righteous. It is the experience of the radical love of God and the radical love of neighbour. 'The Father and I are one,' is the experience of the radical love of God and 'whatever you do to the least of my brothers and sisters you do unto me' is the expression of the radical love of neighbour. It is also the experience of the new covenant in which God writes the Law in the hearts of human beings.

When Jesus had the experience of God at his baptism, God said 'you are my beloved son[61].' God inscribes the Law in the heart of Jesus. God did not reveal what Jesus should do or not do, but who he was.

It is the birth of a new human consciousness, a universal mind, in which a person can say 'I am the way, the truth and the life'. It is the descending of the spirit of God which transforms our humanity and creation. It is the experience of new-heaven and new-earth. It is transcending our relationship with God as creatures–and realizing ourselves as the sons and daughters of God. It is also a freeing from the God of history, the God of Abraham, Isaac and Jacob and an experiencing of the God of eternity, 'I am who I am (Ex.3.14)[62].'

Before Jesus proclaimed this good news he had to find it within his own life. What he realized within, he proclaimed to others. Jesus told his disciples, 'go into the whole world and proclaim the good news to the whole creation[63]'. They have to proclaim the good news that God is everywhere and everyone, that everything is in God, and that humanity is ultimately one with God. This good news has to be proclaimed to the whole creation and not only to human beings: all creatures are the manifestations of God. The dignity of human beings is that they are greater than religions and that they have the truth within themselves. They are invited to realize this truth through repentance–a process of inner purification through which human beings come to this truth, to their true self. If they do not do that, then they live in ignorance and they live from false identity and waste their entire life.

How Did Jesus find the kingdom?

Jesus had many important moments in his life. We can discern four important moments before his crucifixion and resurrection. The first moment was his birth as a human being to Mary, his physical mother. In that sense he was fully human being. The second moment was the day of his circumcision, on which he entered into the collective consciousness of Judaism. He became a Jew, a hundred per cent Jew. As a Jew he might have said that Judaism was his way, his truth and his life, as he was in the womb of Judaism. He related with God as the God of Abraham, Isaac and Jacob, his ancestors. In this stage religion is greater than human beings.

The third moment was his baptismal experience in which he came out of the womb of religion (all religions) and entered the universal presence of God. In this experience he realized that God was everywhere, and everyone and everything was in God. He also inaugurated the new covenant in which God wrote the Law in his heart: 'you are my beloved Son' (Lk.3.21-22). Now Jesus' consciousness is no longer confined to his religion but he becomes a universal person in which Jews and Gentiles (the whole of humanity) are united. Now he says 'I am the way, the truth and the life'. When he was in Judaism, his religion was his way, truth and the life, but now he himself is the way, the truth and the life. In the first (old) covenant religion is the way, the truth and the life but in the new covenant universal consciousness is the way, the truth and the life.

The fourth moment was when he realized that the Father (God) and he were one. In this level God is the way, the truth and the life. With this experience Jesus' ascending journey came to an end–and he felt the mission to communicate this good news to humanity, in particular to his spiritual tradition, and invite people to enter this experience through repentance.

So Jesus began his life journey as an individual, and then entered the collective consciousness of Judaism, from there he moved into the universal consciousness (Son of God), and from there into the divine consciousness. This is the way that Jesus discovered the kingdom of God. The statement of Jesus 'I am the way, the truth and the life' belongs neither to the first level, nor to the second level but can belong either to the third level or to the fourth If Jesus makes this statement as an individual then Jesus, the individual, becomes the way, the truth and the life and everyone has to believe in Jesus, the individual, to be saved. If Jesus makes this statement as a Jew, in the collective consciousness, then Judaism becomes the way, the truth and the life and everyone is invited to become a Jew to be saved. Certainly Jesus was not making this statement as an individual or as a Jew. He was speaking from the universal consciousness and probably from the divine consciousness. The universal consciousness is not an individual or religion, but embraces individuals and religions and transcends them. In this consciousness the way is within him. He is initiating the new covenant.

This new covenant has two aspects: freedom from the past and freedom from the future. It is freedom from the past because Jesus does not follow any person or any belief from the past. If he follows anyone from the past or any belief from the past then that person or that belief becomes the way, the truth and the life, and he cannot say that he is the way, the truth and the life. Jesus even said 'before Abraham was

I am'. This 'I am' is universal I am (not divine I AM). The universal consciousness is free from the past and gives freedom to the future. As it does not follow anyone from the past it does not become a way to the future so that the future remains original and creative. Persons in the future can say like Jesus 'I am the way, the truth and the life'. If they say that Jesus is the way, the truth and the life, then the future is giving continuity to the past and no longer living in the eternal present–to say 'I am the way, the truth and the life' is to live in the eternal present, eternal now, in which a person becomes the vehicle of divine eternity and not a vehicle of the past or the future.

The virgin birth symbolizes this birth of eternity in which the present is free from the past (Joseph) and open to eternity. It gives birth to the indwelling presence of God in which a person says 'I am in God and God is in me'. It also gives birth to universal consciousness in which a person lives for the welfare of all.

A person who lives for himself or herself needs a religion to guide him/her. A person who lives for all does not need a religion, a scripture, an authority. He himself or she herself becomes the way, the truth and life. Jesus said, 'it is written in your Law but I say unto you…[64]' He had authority even over the sacred scriptures. Jesus also said, 'no one comes to the Father except through me'. This means that no one can come to the experience which Jesus had, in which he could say 'I am the way, the truth and the life' and 'the Father and I are one' unless they go through the same way through which Jesus arrived at it. What was the way? It is a journey from individual consciousness to collective consciousness, from collective consciousness to universal consciousness, and from universal to divine consciousness. This is the way through which Jesus came to it and this is the way for everyone.

The Way Jesus Proposed

Even though Jesus said that he was the way, the truth and the life, he also proposed a way through which people can enter the kingdom of God. This way is one but Jesus described it varyingly: the path of repentance, the path of rebirth, the path of becoming like little children, the path of losing oneself, the path of dying, the path of growing, the path of searching, and the path of grace...

The Path of Repentance:

Jesus said, 'the kingdom of God is at hand, repent[65]', or 'repent, for the kingdom of heaven is at hand[66].' The way of repentance is the way of growth. If we take the journey of Jesus from the individual to the divine, repentance is part of this journey. If a person is in individual consciousness, repentance is to enter collective consciousness (religions). If a person is in collective consciousness repentance is to enter universal consciousness. If a person is in universal consciousness repentance is to enter divine consciousness. When Jesus used the word 'repent' he was inviting his listeners to grow beyond their collective consciousness and enter into the universal consciousness and from there to the divine. His listeners were already in the collective consciousness of Judaism. The baptismal experience of Jesus is a kind of repentance in the life of Jesus. It is the transition from the collective consciousness into the universal consciousness. Christian baptism is an entry into the collective consciousness. It is like the circumcision of Jesus through which he entered Jewish collective consciousness. Repentance is not a one-day business, it is a continuous growth in our relationship with God.

The Path of Rebirth:

Jesus told Nicodemus, 'unless you are born again you cannot enter the kingdom of heaven[67].' Nicodemus took this to mean he had to go back into the womb of his physical mother. Impossible, of course. But Jesus was referring to the collective womb of his religion. Nicodemus was in the womb of his religion. He needed to come out of his religious womb and enter in the universal presence of God, to live in the eternal present. 'The wind blows where it wills but you do not know from where it comes and you do not know where it goes, so it is with everyone who is born of the spirit' (Jn.3.8), said Jesus. It is freedom from past and freedom from future. If a person is in an individual womb, he/she has to come out of it and enter the collective womb. If a person is in the collective womb he/she has to come out of it and enter the universal womb of God. If a person is in the universal womb he/she has to enter the unitary womb of God. In every level there is rebirth.

The Path of Becoming like Little Children.

Jesus said, 'unless you become like little children you cannot enter the kingdom of heaven[68].' This statement has to be understood in different levels. Jesus is not saying that everyone should become children physically, which is impossible. A person who is 35 years old cannot become 5 years old physically. A person who lives in a religious identity acquires the age of that religion in the sense that he/she is giving continuity to the tradition which began in the past. For example Christianity began 2013 years ago. So Christians are connected to that time and they are giving continuity to that vision which began 2013 years ago. Actually it is Christianity which is 2013 years old which is living in and through the individuals. Individuals come and go like leaves on a branch, but the branch continues. In that sense we can say Christians are 2013 years old. How can they become little children? They cannot become children as long as they are used by their religion. Only when they come out of the womb of their religion can they enter into the universal consciousness in which their age is just-born. They become like little children.

If we come out of the womb of religion, which belongs to time, then we enter the universal presence of God. We enter the eternal now. In this stage a person is a just-born child. There is a difference between a child physically and a child spiritually. The physical child is innocent and ignorant and the spiritual child is innocent, because it is free from past and future, but also wise as it sees the limitations of past. One can go a little further and realize one's unity with God and become an eternal childlike God. God is ancient but he/she is also an eternal child. So when Jesus invited people to become like little children, he was inviting them to realize their unity with God, which is the kingdom of God.

The Path of Losing One's Self:
Jesus said, 'whoever chooses to save his life (self) shall lose it, and whoever will lose his life (self) shall find it'. This losing and gaining has to be understood in different levels. If we are willing to lose or give up our individual self we will gain our collective self. If we are willing to lose our collective self we will gain our universal self. If we are willing to lose our universal self we will gain our divine self. It is by losing our lower self that we will gain our higher self. If we cling to our lower selves, the individual and collective, we will lose our higher self. So Jesus invited people to lose their lower selves in order to find that higher self, which is finding the kingdom of God.

The Path of Dying:

Jesus said, 'unless a grain of wheat falls into the ground and dies it remains alone but when it dies it gives a mighty harvest[69].' This statement may have different interpretations. One way of interpreting is that it is by dying we move towards the kingdom of God. Again this dying may have many levels. A person, who lives for himself/herself, dies for himself/herself. If a person dies to his/her individual living then he/she may live for his religious community. If a person is living for his/her religion, when this person dies he/she dies to his/her religion, to his/her religious identity, and this person can live for all humanity. So when a person lives for all humanity this person's death is also for all humanity. If a person is willing to die even to the universal identity then the person enters into God and lives like God. So the more we die, the more fruitful our life becomes. It is through continuous dying that we enter the kingdom of God. Jesus did not live only for himself or for his religion, he lived for all, not only for the present-day people but also for the past people and the people of the future. It is for this reason that his death is for all. He is the saviour of the whole of humanity and creation. Only a person, who lives for all, dies for all.

The Path of Growth:

Jesus said, 'the kingdom of God is like a mustard seed. It is the smallest of all seeds. But when it grows it becomes so big that the birds of the air will come and make their nests in it[70].' The seed is the symbol of our limited and individual consciousness. Our individual consciousness has to grow into divine consciousness in which there is a place for all individuals and collective consciousness (religions), represented by the nests. The kingdom of God does not exclude any individual or religion, but transcends them and embraces them. It also invites individuals and collective consciousness to grow into divine consciousness. It is by growing continuously from our limited boundaries into the space without boundaries that we enter the kingdom of God.

The Path of Seeking:

Jesus said, 'the kingdom of God is like a merchant in search of pearls. When he found a pearl of great value, he sold everything and bought that pearl[71].' Here the merchant was a seeker. He was searching and in his search he found the precious pearl. Jesus also said, 'first of all seek you the kingdom of God and its righteousness and all things will be given unto you'.[72] To become a seeker is a very important stage in our spiritual evolution. It is not sufficient to remain as believers and followers—we must become the seeker of the kingdom. The precious pearl is our true self, our divine self. When we come across our true self, then we give up our finite self, the ego. The kingdom of God is the highest divine-human relationship. It is the experience of our unity with God and of our living from that unity that enables a person to say that it is no longer he/she that lives but God lives in him/her.

The Path of Grace:

Jesus said, 'the kingdom of God is like a man who found treasure in the field. He buried it again, went home, sold everything and bought that field'.[73] This man was doing his usual daily work in someone's field. As a surprise he found the treasure. He was not expecting it. Since the land does not belong to him and the treasure was more valuable than all his property, he joyfully sold everything and bought that field. The treasure in the field is the symbol of our true self, our divine self. The property he sold is the symbol of our finite self. When we find our true self we discover that our finite self is nothing in comparison to it. We give it up joyfully and hold to our true self. It is renouncing our ego and accepting our true self without a choice. This giving up can be described as positive renunciation. This discovery came to the person as a surprise, as grace. Of course our spiritual journey is completely a grace of God. God may lead us through specific ways, techniques, structures and religions but he/she is not bound by any of these. His/her grace can manifest outside established structures and religions that he/she has revealed. It can come even without being asked for. It is the expression of the unconditional love of God.

There is Only One Way to God

What we discover from the above explanation is that Jesus is proposing only one way to God: it is to renounce our ego or to expand our ego. Both 'renouncing' and 'expanding' are one and the same. It is renouncing our individual ego for the sake of collective ego, renouncing collective ego for the sake of universal ego, and renouncing universal ego for the sake of divine ego. The more we renounce the more we expand. The word 'renouncing' has a negative connotation. So it is better to use the word 'expanding'. It is growth–a mustard seed growing into a tree. The purpose of every religion, every spiritual practice and every scripture is to help human beings to expand or renounce their ego. The danger comes only when people stop growing and confine themselves to their individual ways or collective ways. Then these religions and techniques, instead of helping people free themselves from their egos, imprison them in their egos.

This 'expanding of our ego' also implies growing in our relationship with God. It is growing from creatures into sons and daughters of God, and from that point realizing our unity with God.

In individual identities and collective identities we may have plurality of relationships with God: each individual relates with God in a unique way and each spiritual tradition relates with God in a unique way. Rig Veda declares that Truth (God) is one and sages call it by many names; Sri Krishna teaches Arjuna, 'in whatever way people worship me in the same way I fulfil their desires (accept and bless them)'. These statements are very suitable to this level. This level creates individual pluralism and collective or religious pluralism, however. It also creates divisions and conflict between different ways and religions. There is no permanent solution at this level for the unity of humankind. Inter-religious dialogue cannot achieve much. It becomes ineffective. It asks for tolerance, acceptance of the other and learning to coexist.

In universal consciousness a person transcends all ways and means, and experiences the indwelling presence of God. Here a person declares 'I am the way, the truth and the life'. This person lives for the welfare of the whole world. The Bhagavat Gita speaks of a wise person who works unselfishly for the welfare of the whole world (Gita. 3.25). In the biblical tradition it is the experience of the new covenant. Here a person transcends individual pluralism and collective or religious pluralism and discovers the essential unity of humanity. Here unity is not based on the spiritual practices or belief structures, which are artificial, but on our human nature. It is the discovery of the image and likeness of God, which is like a pure mirror and in which God reflects in his/her fullness. In discovering our essential nature all the boundaries disappear. A person can still grow further and discover essential unity with God and declare, 'God and I are one' or God alone is. Jesus said, 'the Father and I are one'.

Even though Sri Krishna told Arjuna that 'in whatever way people worship me in the same way I fulfil their desires (accept and bless them)', he also told him 'abandon all spiritual paths (dharmas) and surrender to me, I will deliver you from all your sins.'[74] This reminds us of the statement of Jesus, 'come to me all you who labour and are burdened of heart and I will give you rest; take my yoke upon you and learn from me for I am meek and humble of heart and you will find rest for your souls; for my yoke is easy and my burden is light'.

Abandoning all spiritual paths means abandoning our ego. It is our ego that needs spiritual paths and it is our ego that creates spiritual paths. In this surrender of the ego one discovers one's original self and enters the universal presence of God where sin can never enter. But this surrender is possible only when a person realizes the limitations of all spiritual paths to free one from sins. Even though Rig Veda says that Truth or God is one but sages describe it in many ways, the Upanishads go one step further and declare 'Aham Brahmasmi',[75] I am Brahman or God, and 'Tat Tvam ASI',[76] You are Brahman or God. It is not only that Truth or God is one but also that human beings are ultimately one with that one Truth or God. It is going beyond individual pluralism, collective pluralism and universal consciousness. This is the liberating message of the Upanishads. Only in that experience do we arrive at the final destiny of our spiritual journey, our ultimate rest, our ultimate fulfilment and our inner peace. It is only there that we find our infinite being, infinite consciousness, and infinite bliss: Saccidananda.

We can use two images to describe this spiritual evolution: a mountain and a tree.

The Way of a Mountain

Many spiritual traditions have their temples built on the top of a hill or a mountain. They are places of pilgrimage. Our spiritual journey can be seen as a journey from the bottom of a mountain to the top of a mountain. As individuals we each begin our journey at the bottom of the hill at different starting points. As we move higher and higher we come closer and closer and our journey becomes collective. As we move still higher we almost become one. Finally when we reach the top of the hill we realize our unity with God. So it is really a journey from individual identity to divine identity. As we climb higher and higher we are expanding our identity or consciousness. It is also a process of renouncing our lower forms of ego and growing into higher levels of ego. It is a journey from multiplicity into unity.

There are some shelters built along the way if pilgrims would like to rest for a while. These shelters are our belief structures, either individual or collective. There are our resting places but they are not permanent settlements. If we settle down in these temporary shelters, then we stop our spiritual journey or evolution. When Abraham was called by God to leave everything and go to the place which God would reveal to him, it is said that he was living in tents. A tent is a temporary shelter erected at the end of the day for rest, sustenance and sleep–and destined to be removed when a person starts his or her journey the next day. It is the same with our spiritual journey. We may erect individual tents or collective tents on the mountain but we should not settle in them for good. Our goal is to reach the top of the mountain. What is consoling on this journey is that God or truth is there from the bottom of the mountain to the top of the mountain. Everyone is on the path of God and no one is outside God. This is what Sri Krishna meant when he told Arjuna, 'in every way people follow my path' (Gita. 4.11). But ultimately one has to go beyond all the paths, beyond ego. It is also a journey in humility. The more a person grows the more humble that person becomes. Only in the individual level and the collective level can there be a sense of superiority or inferiority but in the universal level and the unitary level a person becomes very humble–because at these levels others do not exist essentially, only functionally. Jesus said, 'the Father and I are one' and then he washed the feet of his disciples, an act of great humility.

The Way of a Tree:
Another image is the tree. A tree has leaves, branches, trunk and roots. Leaves represent our individual identities. The branches represent our collective identities. The trunk represents our universal identity, and roots represent our divine identity. At the level of leaves we have pluralistic relationships with God: individual pluralism. At the level of branches we have pluralistic belief structures: religious pluralism. At the level of the trunk we have essential unity of humanity. We transcend individual pluralism and religious pluralism. At the level of roots we have our oneness with God. A tree represents the whole truth. It contains all levels of truth. In that sense no one is outside the tree, outside the truth. At the level of leaves truth is fragmented into individuals. At the level of branches it is fragmented into belief structures. At the level of the trunk it is the fragmentation of creator and creation. At the level of roots it is all embracing. We see one truth, one way and one life. When Jesus said, 'I am the way, the truth and the life', he was saying that he embodied the fullness of Truth. He was the whole Tree. He contained within him all levels of truth. He was the beginning and the end, the Alpha and the Omega. He invited everyone to grow from the fragmented truth into the fullness of truth. It is a journey from many to one, from diversity to unity.

The Inclusive Way of Christ

In conclusion, the way of Jesus is not *a way* among many other ways to God. It is not the *only way* that excludes all other ways to God; neither is it *the perfect way* among the imperfect ways. It is *the way* that includes or embraces all the other ways to God–dynamically. It includes all individual ways to God (the leaves–individual pluralism) but invites them to recognize the need of branches, collective ways.

It includes all collective ways (the branches–religious pluralism) but invites them to recognize the need of the trunk–universal way. The universal way is the end of individual ways and collective ways.

Finally this way invites everyone to move beyond the universal way into the divine way where a person says: God is the only way, only truth and only life. This is the way of the tree.

This way is not only ascending to unity but also descending back to diversity. It is not only reaching to the top of the mountain but also returning to the bottom of the mountain. It is not only going to the roots but also coming back to the leaves. It is not only vertical growth but also horizontal. It is growing into the radical love of God and the radical love of neighbour. As one grows higher into the love of God one also expands into the love of neighbour.

Christianity so far has interpreted Christ's message in a very exclusive way. This interpretation does not do justice to his universal and inclusive message. Christianity today must rediscover the inclusive message of Christ and thus help contribute to the search for peace in the world.

13.
INTEGRAL DYNAMIC MONOTHEISM

All philosophies, all ideologies, all scriptures, all religions and all prophets and sages tell us two important things: who we are and how we have to live our life in this world of time and space.

The identity a person has determines the way a person lives his or her life. In this paper we will limit our search to the religious level: what do the religions say we are and how should we live our life? Nowadays it is common to divide religions into two important categories (not in an absolute sense): the Wisdom Tradition and the Prophetic Tradition. Religions like Hinduism, Buddhism and Jainism belong to the Wisdom Tradition. They have in common elements like karma, samsara and reincarnation. Religions like Judaism, Christianity and Islam belong to the Prophetic Tradition. These religions are also called Monotheistic Religions as they believe in one God.

We will focus our reflection on the Monotheistic Religions[77] and Hinduism.

PROPHETIC MONOTHEISM

According to traditional Judaism[78], God is the creator and human beings are creatures of God. God creates creation and human beings out of nothing. There is a gulf between God and human beings. There is an essential difference between them. Human beings cannot see God face to face. God is the liberator and saviour. He guides his people via the prophets. He reveals his will through the commandments. The Torah reveals the will of God and people have to follow it. To obey the Torah is to obey God. One has to submit one's will and intellect to the will of God and one has to be faithful and loyal to God. Jews consider themselves to be specially chosen by God. So according to Judaism human beings are creatures of God. They are expected to live a moral life according to the will of God.

According to traditional Christianity[79] God is the creator and human beings are creatures of God. There is an essential difference between God and human beings. God revealed his will through the prophets in the Old Testament and he revealed his final will in the person of Jesus Christ. Jesus Christ is the only Son of God. He is the incarnation of the third person of the Holy Trinity. He is the only way, the truth, the life. One has to believe in Jesus Christ as the only Son of God and become a Christian to be saved. Some insist only on believing in Christ as the saviour to be saved and others underline believing in Christ to which they add living a moral life and doing good works. If one lives a good life one will go to heaven and if one lives a bad life one will go to hell after death.

According to traditional Islam[80] God is the creator and human beings are creatures of God. There is an essential difference between God and creation. God revealed his will through the prophets in the

Old testaments and in Jesus Christ, but he revealed his final will in the Holy Koran through Prophet Muhammad. Hence the Koran is the final word of God and Prophet Muhammad is the last prophet. God did not reveal himself but revealed the Koran in which he tells human beings what they should do and what they should not do. The Koran is considered the eternal word of God dictated to Prophet Muhammad. Submission to the will of God revealed in the Koran is necessary for salvation. To obey the Koran is to obey God. If one lives a moral life according to the Koran one will go to heaven and if one does not live a moral life then one will go to hell after one's death.

According to these three religions God is the creator and human beings are creatures of God. The difference between Judaism, Islam and Christianity is the person of Jesus Christ and Trinity. Jews and Muslims do not believe that God is Trinity. They think it violates the unity of God. They do not believe that Jesus Christ is the incarnation of the second person of the Holy Trinity. They do not believe that he is the only Son of God and that he is the only way, the truth and the life. They believe that he is a human being like any other human being. He is a messenger of God or a reformer of Judaism. If he called himself the son of God, it is only in the metaphorical sense that every one is a son or daughter of God.

These three religions are called Monotheistic Religions because they believe that there is only one God and this one God is the creator of the universe. The general expression is that God created this universe out of nothing. There is an essential difference between God and creation which includes human beings. In Christianity exception is made of Jesus Christ–Jesus Christ is not a creature of God but incarnation of God. There is an essential difference between Christ and other human beings.

HINDU MONOTHEISM

The expression 'Hindu Monotheism' may surprise some.

In general Hinduism is described as monism, non-dualism, pantheism and polytheism. But one has to be aware that according to Hinduism there is only one God or absolute Reality (Monotheism); but this God is not the creator–he/she/it manifests creation.

Hinduism does not propose the theory of creation out of nothing. This is the basic difference between Prophetic Monotheism and Hindu Monotheism.

There are three important theological positions in Hinduism[81]. These positions are based on the interpretations given to the teachings of the Upanishads and the Bhagavad-Gita, and the Brahma Sutras, the sacred scriptures of Hinduism. The Upanishads date from the fifth century before Christ and the Bhagavad-Gita, from around the first century before or after Christ[82]. These scriptures did not propose any theological system, the systems came later. The fundamental question of these systems is the relationship between God and creation, God and human beings. In Prophetic Monotheism this question seems to have been resolved with the theory of creation out of nothing. Since Hindu Monotheism does not accept this solution it needs to propose different solutions.

Advaita–Non-duality

The first philosophical system is called Advaita, a system of non-duality proposed by Shankara in the eighth century[83] after Christ. According to him God (Brahman) alone is eternal (sathyam). Creation (Jagat) is an illusion, non-eternal (mithya). It is also described with the famous word Maya. Ultimately the human soul (jivatman) is identical with God (Brahman). This can be explained with the analogy of water (God) and ice. Only water is there. The ice comes from water and melts back to water. But the form of ice does not have an independent existence. It has a beginning and an end. The ice is essentially one with water, though functionally different. The ice does not become water. It is water. But it is not aware that it is water. Because it is solid it imagines that it is a stone. It is in ignorance. It needs to free itself from ignorance and realize that it is water or God.

Shankara proposed the way of wisdom, jnana marga. The paths of devotion (bhakti) and action (karma) can prepare the way but jnana is the ultimate as ignorance can be removed only through wisdom and not by devotion or action as they are not the opposite of ignorance.

For Shankara God or Brahman is nirguna, without qualities. Brahman is impersonal. Human beings are essentially one with God but they are ignorant of this truth. They have to realize this truth. According to him ultimately every human being can say, 'Aham brahmaasmi', I am Brahman, 'God and I are one'. A person who realizes this truth while alive is called jivan muktha, liberated while alive. In general Shankara is considered to be a monist but a better description would be that he is a non-dualist: God and creation are not two independent realities.

Visistaadvaita–Qualified Non-dualism

The second system is called Visistaadvaita, qualified non-dualism, proposed by Ramanuja in the eleventh century after Christ.

He disagreed with Shankara's position regarding the nature of God and creation and human souls. As with Shankara, for Ramanuja God (Brahman) alone is eternal (sathyam). But this God is not nirguna, without qualities–but saguna, with qualities. God is personal. Creation (Jagat) is the manifestation of Brahman (not an illusion, mithya, as with Shankara).

Creation is not created by God–it is emanation from God. God is the material and instrumental cause of creation. Human souls are part of God but not identical with God. There is an essential difference between God and human souls. God has creation together with human souls as his body. The relationship between God and creation is like soul and body, or body and the hair that grows on the body. God and creation are inseparable. Creation is not an illusion, mithya, or Maya. Maya is the creative power of God through which he manifests the creation.

If we take the analogy of water and ice: Brahman is water, ice is the creation and human souls. Ice is not an illusion. It is the manifestation of Brahman. It is the body of Brahman. But there is a subtle difference between God and creation which includes human souls. They are not identical with Brahman.

Ramanuja proposed the way of devotion, bhakti marga. One has to surrender to God through devotion or faith so that God can take responsibility for one's life–one finds peace and joy in this surrender.

There is no human soul merging with God. No one can say, 'God and I are one'. Personal relationship with God is very important. If human soul merges with God then no personal relationship is possible. Human beings can have a personal relationship with God with different aspects like: father and son, husband and wife, protector and protected, physician and patient, sustainer and sustained, sun and lotus, clouds and seeds, supporter and dependent, owner and owned. Ultimate liberation is only after the death of the physical body. In general Ramanuja is considered to be a pantheist. But this may not be correct since he holds that there is a subtle essential difference between God and creation and human souls.

Dvaita-Duality

The third position is called Dvaita, a system of duality, proposed by Madhva in the twelfth century after Christ. He disagreed with both Shankara and Ramanuja regarding the nature of God, creation and human souls–and proposed dualism. Madhva would agree with Shankara and Ramanuja that God alone is eternal (sathyam). According to him God is Brahman and Brahman is Vishnu and his other incarnations. Creation is essentially different form God. Creation is not an illusion (which Shankara professed), neither is it the manifestation of God (Ramanuja). It is not created by God. It is there from the beginning, eternal but essentially different from God. Human souls are essentially different from God.

There is a gulf between God and creation and human beings. The immeasurable power of Lord Vishnu is seen as the efficient cause (the agent) of the universe and the primordial matter (prakrti) is the material cause of the universe. God is personal and has many qualities, saguna. Human soul is essentially different from God. This position keeps human beings somewhat distant from God but strengthens the relationship between each other.

He proposed the path of devotion, bhakti marga, and good works, karma marga. One needs to surrender to God through devotion and do good works. The indwelling presence of God inspires the soul to act and gives reward or punishment accordingly but God is not affected by these actions. According to Madhva human beings are more or less creatures of God (though he may not like to use the word 'creatures' in the sense of being created out of nothing), though essentially different now and after this life. The human soul might come closer to God through devotion but without merging with him. Liberation is the state of attaining maximum joy or sorrow, which is awarded to the soul according to its actions at the end of its spiritual practice, which would be after its death.

These three systems believe that there is only one God, one eternal Reality. In that sense they are monotheistic religions. But they do not believe that this one Reality is a creator. This is the main difference between Prophetic Monotheism and Hindu Monotheism. Many think that Hinduism is polytheistic. In practice it looks like that but Hinduism believes that there is only one God and different gods are either various manifestations of that one God or like the angels in Prophetic Monotheism.

It is interesting to note how human consciousness has fallen from the non-dual experience of God to the dualistic experience: from the Vedic tradition with its climax in the Upanishads in the fifth century before Christ, realizing that human consciousness is one with the divine—to the twelfth century after Christ when Madhva's dualistic understanding predominated, affirming an essential difference between God and human souls.

There are therefore three important concepts of a human being:
- essentially one with God, as per the advaita of Shankara,
- manifestation of God as per visistaadvaita of Ramanuja,
- essentially different from God, as in Judaism, Christianity, and Islam and the dvaita system of Hinduism.

What is common to them all is that there is only one God. In that sense they are all monotheists. The difference is the way human beings relate with that one God.

Some Observations

Prophetic Monotheism reduces human beings into creatures of God and thus closes the door to their realization as the sons and daughters of God and of being one with God. The theory of creation out of nothing is not a very liberating theory as it blocks the spiritual evolution of human consciousness. Shankara opened to creation and human beings the possibility to realize themselves as being one with God. He focused exclusively on human beings' divinity—at the cost of their humanity however. Human existence and relationships appear to have no significance.

Ramanuja attempted to correct this extreme position and give some meaning and purpose to creation and human relationships. He gave creation and human beings the dignity of divine manifestation and divine son-ship and daughtership—but at the cost of their divinity.

Madhva tried to bring God to the level of human beings in all their limitations but it was done at the cost of their divine son-ship and daughter-ship and also their divinity.

The position of Shankara on the nature of creation is very ambiguous. If he really means that creation is an illusion then creation is purposeless. If he means that creation, in the sense of names and forms, is not eternal then there is some meaning to creation and human existence. The names and forms are not eternal but what is within the names and forms is eternal. In that sense creation is also divine in its essence just as human beings are essentially one with the divine in their essence.

In general his system is interpreted to mean that creation is an illusion or Maya. This position does not give any positive role to creation and human beings in the world of time and space. The entire focus is on realizing our divinity and then everything comes to an end.

Ramanuja holds that Brahman is the material and instrumental cause of creation and human souls. In that sense they are essentially one with Brahman though functionally may be different like water and ice. If it is so what prevents human souls from merging with Brahman in the ultimate level? In the same manner as what prevents ice melting into water? It seems that there is some contradiction in his proposition. Madhva holds that creation is completely different from Brahman. He also holds that creation has no beginning as it is eternal.

How can both God and creation be eternal? These three Hindu Monotheistic systems, advaita, visistaadvaita and dvaita, need to integrate the love of neighbour and social transformation, just as the prophetic Monotheistic Religions need to open themselves to a non-dualistic experience with God. There have been many great Hindu mystics, such as Sri Ramakrishna and his disciple Swami Vivekananda, who have tried to integrate the love of God with the love of neighbour and social transformation. So also there have been many mystics in the prophetic religions who opened human consciousness to the non-dualistic experience of God even though they had to face many difficulties from the ecclesiastic authorities.

Jesus Christ: a Prophetic Monotheist or a Hindu Monotheist?

Jesus Christ made statements which do not fit within Prophetic Monotheism. He called God his Father. He said that he was the Son of God. He was in the Father and the Father in him. He came from the Father and returned to the Father. He also claimed that the Father (God) and he were one. His experience of God did not fit within the belief system of Prophetic Monotheism. For Jesus, God was not his creator and he was not a creature. His origin is in eternity. Judaism and Islam reject his claims and consider them blasphemous.

They think that his statements are metaphorical and not metaphysical. Christianity accepts his claims but limits them only to Jesus, not envisaging it as a possibility for every human being. The claims of Jesus are very close to the qualified non-dualistic and non-dualistic systems of Hinduism–they make perfect sense to these two systems. In this way Jesus was more a Hindu Monotheist than a Prophetic Monotheist. In qualified non-dualism and non-dualism these claims are not limited to any one particular individual but a possibility to every human being.

Jesus Christ: a Dualist, a Qualified Non-Dualist or a Non-Dualist?

We are dealing with this question retrospectively. These systems did not exist in Jesus' times. But these systems give us some tools to understand Jesus' experience.

Jesus made three important statements: 'my Father is greater than me', 'I am in the Father and the Father is in me' and 'the Father and I are one'.

The first statement is in accordance with the dualistic system. God is the creator and Jesus is the creature. God is greater than him. The second statement is in accordance with the qualified non-dualistic system. Here the relationship is much more intimate. It is not the relationship of creator and creature. It is the relationship of Father and Son. He is in God and God is in him. It is an experience of mutual indwelling. Still there is some distance between him and the Father. He is not the Father. The third statement is in accordance with the non-dualistic system. The Father and he are one. There is no distance. There is no separation. If we take them all together then it appears Jesus is contradicting himself. If God is greater than him then he cannot say 'I am in the Father and the Father is in me'. If there is a distance between God and Jesus then he cannot say that God and he are one.

We can say that Jesus began his journey with the experience of being a creature (dualist) and experienced God as greater than him according to his spiritual tradition. At the moment of his baptismal experience he went beyond that relationship and realized that he was not a creature but the son of God (qualified non-dualist), the manifestation of God. Later he went even beyond that and realized that he was one with the Father, God (non-dualist). He did not remain exclusively in that non-dual experience however; for as long as he lived in his physical body and in the world of time and space, he permeated between the qualified non-dualistic experience, the dualistic experience and the non-dualistic experience. We cannot put him into any one of these systems.

Integral Dynamic Monotheism

We have seen different types of monotheisms: the simple Monotheism of the Upanishads, which affirms that there is only one God (Brahman, Atman) and the ground of human consciousness is one with that one God; Prophetic Monotheism, which affirms that there is only One God and creation is essentially different; the non-dualistic Monotheism of Shankara which affirms that there is only one God and creation is an illusion or unreal; the qualified non-dualistic Monotheism of Ramanuja, which affirms that there is only one God and creation is his body; and the dualistic Monotheism of Madhva, which affirms that there is only one God and creation also is eternal but essentially different from God.

Jesus' experience does not fit into any of these monotheisms. So I like to describe him—though not to define him—as an Integral Dynamic Monotheist.

The Integral Dynamic Monotheism of Jesus Christ

The Integral Dynamic Monotheism of Jesus can be described in this way:

God alone is. God alone is eternal (sathyam and nithyam).

This God cannot be put into any human categories. It is independent, creative, timeless, peace and love. It is personal, impersonal and beyond. It is like an infinite space and our concepts of it are like houses that we build within the space. It allows the building of houses according to the needs and capacities of the human mind but it always transcends them. Our human mind cannot build a house for the infinite space.

Creation is the manifestation of God: Creation (names and forms) is not an illusion. It is unreal, finite. It has a beginning and an end. It is one with God in being—but different in manifestation, like water and ice, energy and matter. Water and ice are one but different. Energy and matter are one but different manifestations.

Human souls are one with God in their foundation but different in manifestation. Names and forms are like mirrors in which God reflects. Human consciousness is the breath of God breathed in our earthen vessel.[84] When the reflection identifies with the names and the forms it feels it is finite. When it looks into the source then it realizes being one with God. Human souls have the possibility to evolve into different levels and experience God according to their level.

It is Integral:
This monotheism integrates all the systems mentioned above and also other possible systems but transcends each system. God or Truth cannot be put into any system. It is essentially non-dualistic but functionally qualified non-dualistic and dualistic. This monotheism does not exclude any spiritual path but embraces all spiritual paths that help human beings to grow in relationship with God and with neighbours. The spiritual paths of wisdom (jnana), devotion (bhakti) and action (karma) are not seen as exclusive but mutually complementing.

It is Dynamic:
The relationship between God and human souls is not static but dynamic. It is an ascending and descending process. Human souls grow in their relationship with God, from dualistic relationship to qualified non-dualistic relationship and from there into non-dualistic relationship. Then they descend from the non-dualistic state to the qualified non-dualistic state and from there to the dualistic state. When the soul is ascending these levels look like different stages and the human soul feels that it is different from God. But when the soul is descending these stages are transformed into levels of consciousness. One can live all the levels at the same time without any contradiction. In one level there is unity or non-duality and another level there is difference, duality. A useful symbol could be a tree. A tree is one but comprises functional differences: leaves, branches, trunk and the roots.

Growing into the Love of God and Love of Neighbour:
In this monotheism the focus is on growing into the love of God and love of neighbour. 'The Father and I are one'[85] and 'whatever you do to the least of my brothers and sisters that you do unto me'[86] are the two pillars of this monotheism.

One has to begin with the dualistic love of God and love of neighbour in which a person says: God is my creator, I am a creature and my neighbour is another creature of God. Then grow into the qualified non-dualistic love of God and love of neighbour in which a person says: God is my Father, I am a manifestation of God and my neighbour is another manifestation of God. And finally arrive at the non-dualistic love of God and love of neighbour in which only God is—my Real self is God (aham Brahma asmi) and the Real self of my neighbour is also God (tatvamasi). It is God loving God.

To realize our oneness with God in our deepest level and live dualistically in our relationships with one another in the world of time and space, sharing love and compassion, is perhaps the greatest miracle of life.

14.
THE FORMLESS AND THE FORMS

Like bubbles on the surface of water
All forms come from the Formless
And all dissolve into it!
By knowing that we are both
We will find peace in our hearts.
Let there be a dance of love between forms.

Atmajyothi, which means light of Atman, was a great sage. She was srutistothra, learned in the sacred scriptures, and brahmanista, established in Brahman, the Divine Self. She taught that there is only one absolute Reality and all names and forms come from that one Reality and disappear into it. The names and forms are like waves or bubbles that appear on the surface of an ocean and disappear into it. She taught that the one Reality manifests names and forms in order to know its own attributes in relationships. Manifesting creation is the dance of the divine. The purpose of our human existence is to discover our unity with that one Reality and unfold the attributes of love and compassion at the level of names and forms in our relationships. Human existence is a dance in relationships.

Aranya was an ardent seeker of Atman, the Ultimate Reality. She changed her name into Atmanvesi, which means seeker of Atman. She went to Atmajyothi with love and reverence to be her spiritual student. She was twelve years old. She lived with her teacher for twelve years. Atmajyothi taught her all the scriptures and sciences. Atmanvesi became srutistothra, expert in all the spiritual sciences. Atmajyothi told her: 'my daughter, I have taught you everything I know and now it is time for you to go home.' Atmanvesi thanked her teacher and went home full of gratitude.

One day Atmanvesi's mother asked her: 'my child, tell me what you have learnt about Atman.' Atmanvesi began to repeat to her mother what she had learnt by heart from the scriptures during the twelve years of her stay with her teacher. But her mother told her: 'my child, you are telling me your knowledge about Atman. What I want from you is wisdom, the essence of your learning.' 'I don't understand Mama,' answered Atmanvesi. Her mother said: 'my child, go back to your teacher and ask her two questions: firstly, what is the relationship between Atman and its manifestation, between the formless and the forms, between the Infinite and the finite? Secondly, what is the purpose of our human existence?'

Atmanvesi went back to Atmajyothi with love and respect and stayed with her for a year. Afterwards she asked her: 'mother, explain to me the relationship between Atman and its manifestation, between the formless and the forms, between the Infinite and the finite?'

Atmajyothi said, 'my daughter, bring a piece of paper'. Atmanvesi did so. 'Make a boat out of it, my daughter.' Atmanvesi made a boat out of the paper. 'What do you see, my daughter?' asked Atmajyothi. 'I see a boat,' said Atmanvesi. 'Now dismantle the boat, my daughter,' said Atmajyothi. 'Now what do you see, my daughter?' she asked. 'I see only paper, mother,' replied Atmanvesi. 'Where is the boat, my daughter?' asked Atmajyothi. Atmanvesi realized that the boat was only a form that came from the paper and disappeared into it. Paper was the only reality. Atmajyothi said, 'my daughter, you are the paper and you are the boat. You are the formless and you are the forms that appear and disappear.' 'Teach me more, mother,' asked Atmanvesi.

Atmajyothi took Atmanvesi to a beach where children were playing in the sand. The children were making many forms out of the sand. They were making shapes of animals, humans and houses. Atmajyothi and Atmanvesi sat on the ground watching the children play. At the end they dismantled all the forms they had made and went home. Atmajyothi asked Atmanvesi: 'where are all the forms the children made?' Atmanvesi realized that sand was the only reality and all the forms came from it and disappeared into it. Atmajyothi said to Atmanvesi: 'my daughter, just as all the forms came from the sand and disappeared into it, so all the forms come from Atman and disappear into it. You are Atman and you are the forms that come from Atman.' 'Explain more to me, mother,' said Atmanvesi. 'So be it, my daughter,' replied Atmajyothi.

Atmajyothi told her student: 'daughter, bring me a glass of water.' Atmanvesi brought a glass of water and said, 'here is a glass of water, mother.' 'My daughter, place this water in the freezer and bring the glass to me tomorrow morning,' said Atmajyothi. Atmanvesi did as she was commanded and brought the glass to her teacher the next morning. 'What do you see in the glass, my daughter?' asked the teacher. 'I see an ice cube, mother,' replied Atmanvesi. 'Place the glass under the sun, my daughter.' Atmanvesi placed the glass under the sun until the ice melted. 'What do you see, my daughter?' asked Atmajyothi. 'I see only water, mother,' replied the student. 'Where is the ice, my daughter?' asked Atmajyothi. Atmanvesi realized the truth that the form of ice came from water and disappeared into it. Only the water is real and ice is only the name and the form that appeared and disappeared. Atmanvesi said to her teacher: 'Mother, I realize that there is only one eternal reality and it has two aspects: eternal and temporal. Formless is its eternal aspect and names and forms are its temporal aspect. Names and forms come from the eternal and disappear into it. I am the eternal and the temporal, the formless and the forms, the infinite and the finite.'

On that day Atmanvesi went to her room peacefully. Next day, she came to her teacher and asked: 'mother I know that there is only one eternal Reality and all forms come from that reality and I am that Reality. But what is the purpose of it all? Is there any meaning and significance to this manifestation?'

Atmajyothi said: 'my daughter, go to the nearby village and make a tour in the village and tell me what you see there.' Atmanvesi went to the nearby village. In the first house she saw a young woman feeding her child. She found both the mother and the child in ecstasy. In the second house she saw a young man bathing his sick father. The young man's face was filled with tenderness and affection. The father's face was filled with gratitude. In the next house she saw a young man and woman in each other's embrace, oblivious of their surroundings. Next she saw on the street a woman carrying her invalid child on her back. There was no discomfort on her face. In the next house she saw a woman giving food to a beggar. In the next house she saw a man welcoming a stranger to stay in his house. Wherever she looked she saw two things: giving and receiving.

Atmanvesi returned to Atmajyothi, her face radiating with joy as if she had found her answer. Atmajyothi asked Atmanvesi: 'my daughter, what did you see?' Atmanvesi replied: 'mother, I realize that the primary purpose of my human existence is to realize that I am the one eternal Reality and that I am the temporal; I am the formless and I am the forms; I am the infinite and I am the finite. I have to unfold love and compassion at the level of my names and forms. I am the giver and I am also the receiver. It is in this giving and receiving that I unfold my being and know myself. It is for this reason that the forms come from me and disappear into me.'

Atmajyothi was very happy and said: 'my daughter, now you can go home since you have seen the truth. You are not only srutistothra, expert in scriptures, but also brahmanista, established in Brahman-Atman. I admire your eagerness and dedication for truth. May I find another student like you!'

Atmanvesi fell at the feet of her teacher and said: 'mother, bless me.' Atmajyothi raised Atmanvesi with her arms, placed her hands on her head and blessed her: 'my daughter, may you be firmly established in your realization! May you always be aware of the play of the forms on the formless! May you continuously see all forms as your forms! May you manifest love and compassion in your relationships! May you help many to see the Light of Truth! From now on your name will not be Atmanvesi but it will be Atmajyothi, as you have seen the light of Truth-Atman.

Aranya became Atmanvesi and Atmanvesi became Atmajyothi. Atmajyothi became a great sage and master and helped many to become like her.

May the world be full of people like Atmajyothi and Aranya!

15.
BEARING WITHNESS TO THE TRUTH

'May they all be one, just as, Father, you are in me and I am in you, so that they all may be in us so that they world may believe it was you who sent me'

Jn. 17.21

'I came into the world to bear witness to the Truth,' Jesus told Pilate. 'What is truth?' Pilate answered. [87]
'What is truth?...' Our eternal question. What is the truth that Jesus came to reveal? What is the truth that Jesus bore witness to?

Jesus did not give any answer. He was silent. It may be the silence of someone who stands in front of an infinite ocean of truth and has no adequate words to describe it. It may be the silence of someone who knows that truth is something alive, something dynamic and that cannot be defined, that cannot be put into a box because to define the truth is to kill it. It may be the silence of a modest person who knows that he is the embodiment of truth but hesitates to say it for fear of being misunderstood or labelled as presumptuous. It may be the silence of a prudent person who considers that it is not an appropriate moment to speak. It may be the silence of someone who knows that the person who asked the question is not really interested in knowing truth and it will be a futile exercise to tell him about it. Or it may be the silence of a loving and compassionate one who gives freedom to each one of us to complete this silence according to each person's growth and understanding of truth. One can speculate about this silence in so many ways. I would like to propose that the truth that Jesus Christ came to reveal is the kingdom of God or reign of God.

The Kingdom of God is Radical Love

Jesus did not define the kingdom of God but only described it in many ways. We can say that the kingdom of God is the experience of the unconditional love of God. It is the transformation of all our actions into actions of God. It is the realization that creation is the manifestation of God. It is the experience of the radical love of God and the radical love of neighbour. Jesus grew into one hundred per cent love of God and hundred per cent love of neighbour. In him, the love of God and the love of neighbour reached their fullness. When Jesus said, 'the Father and I are one,'[88] he was revealing the radical love of God. When he said that 'whatever you do to the least of my brothers and sisters that you do unto me',[89] he was revealing the radical love of neighbour. Jesus is one with God and one with every human being and creation; he is the kingdom of God. He invited everyone to grow into the kingdom of God.

The Purpose of Revelation

The purpose of revelation is to reveal who human beings are–and how they need to live their lives in this world of time and space. Revelation is not something static but dynamic. The manner in which God reveals to human beings depends also on their intellectual, psychological, scientific and emotional conditions. Revelation is not necessarily limited to that which comes from above but can extend to that which comes from within–hence through the inner process of self-enquiry.

Two Spiritual Traditions–Vedic and Biblical

It is common today to divide spiritual traditions into two categories: the wisdom tradition and the prophetic tradition. Religions like Hinduism, Buddhism, Jainism and Taoism belong to the wisdom tradition. Religions like Judaism, Christianity, Islam, and Baha'i, belong to the prophetic tradition.[90] In the wisdom tradition revelation is something that human beings discover through their profound spiritual enquiry–there is an inner journey, inner conquest, inner purification and self-realization. This process is guided by the inherent grace present in every human being.

In the prophetic tradition revelation is something that God reveals to a person or persons directly or through an angel. Here grace is experienced as if coming from above, external. In the wisdom religions the focus is on interior liberation or self-realization. In the prophetic religions the focus is on the love of God and love of neighbour. Each way of understanding has its uniqueness but also its limitations. The ideal is the union of these two.

I would like to propose that there are different levels and different types of revelation both in the wisdom and the prophetic traditions. These revelations are basically a continuous growth in divine-human relationship and human-human relationship. Here, we shall take Hinduism, from the Vedic tradition, as a model of the wisdom tradition and Christianity, from the Biblical tradition, as the sample of the prophetic tradition.

The Vedic Tradition

The Vedic tradition is based on the Four Vedas, which are considered to be sacred scriptures of Hinduism. Upanishads are the concluding portion of the Vedas hence they are often called Vedanta. The Vedas are considered to be eternal and without any human origin. They are called sruti. The seers or sages discovered them in their deep meditation. They are not understood as revealed, in the manner of the Commandments given by God to Moses on Mount Sinai. They are like truths discovered by scientists through their research. The only difference is that scientists look outside whereas seers look within. In the Vedas we discover that the divine-human relationship grew continuously and culminated in the Upanishads and integrated in the Bhagavat Gita.

The relationship between God and human beings was first expressed in nature-worship in which natural powers like water, fire, air and sky are seen as divine. Human beings were completely dependent on them and they were at their mercy for their survival. Later this nature-worship developed into polytheism when humans began to personify the natural powers and worshipped them as persons. Water becomes AP or Varuna, fire becomes Agni, air becomes Vayu and sky becomes Indra, the god of the sky. This polytheism developed into henotheism[91] in which one particular God became a kind of leader to other gods.

Henotheism developed into monotheism in which one supreme God was affirmed: *ekam sat vipra bahuthi vadanti*, Truth (God) is one but sages describe it by many names.[92] But their enquiry did not stop with monotheism. They went further in questioning the relationship of creation with that one God since they did not accept the theory of creation out of nothing. They held that creation is not a creature of God but a manifestation of God. God is like a spider and creation is like the web that comes from the spider. Since creation comes from God it is sacred. They declared that everything is the manifestation of Brahman or God, *sarvam khalvidham Brahma*.

Their search went still further and they realized that human consciousness is ultimately one with God. Atman is Brahman. Atman[93] is the ground of the human consciousness and Brahman is the ground of the universe. This experience is described with famous statements such as *aham Brahma asmi* (I am Brahman) and *tatvamasi* (You are That, Brahman). This is the achievement of the Upanishad sages. This experience is often described as advaita or non-dualism. It means that Brahman (God) and creation are not two independent realities. Brahman is *sat* (real or eternal) and creation is *a-sat* (unreal or not eternal). Sat is that which exists by itself and a-sat is that whose existence is dependent on something else. God is sat and creation is a-sat because its existence is dependent on God. Some interpret this experience as monism in the sense that God alone is there and creation is an illusion. But the Upanishad sages were not monists, they were non-dualists. They did not use the word 'illusion' but a-sat, not eternal. It was Shankara who used the word 'mithya', which some translate as 'illusion'. In fact it is not possible to put Vedic seers in any particular system. They just communicated their experiences as they progressed in their spiritual evolution. The labels are assigned by their observers.

As human consciousness progressed the lower relationships were not rejected but allowed to exist as a kind of ladder to spiritual evolution.

The Bhagavat Gita-Spiritual Genius

During the time of the Bhagavat Gita there were many spiritual paths and ideologies, sometimes in conflict with one another. The author of the Bhagavat Gita was a spiritual genius as he was able to accommodate every spiritual path and ideology and proposed his own vision of Love in which the path of wisdom and action are united. He brought together both the human and the divine, Arjuna and Krishna. Human will becomes a vehicle of divine will. Arjuna finally says 'thy will be done' (Gita.18.73). It was an extraordinary achievement and the work of grace. The impersonal God of the Upanishads becomes a personal God. A God who does not speak in the Upanishads speaks in the Bhagavat Gita. Krishna speaks non-stop for eighteen chapters in the middle of the battlefield. Even though there is much emphasis on the love of God and selfless action, there is not much emphasis on the love of neighbour and socially transformative action. Since it was written in the context of a battlefield its tone is very much focused on action that comes from wisdom. The external battle is taken as the symbol of inner spiritual battle in which there is a fight between the good (Pandavas) and the bad (Kauravas). Ultimately the good with the help of God (Krishna) wins the battle.

Three Theological Systems

Later three main theological systems were developed based on the teachings of the Upanishads, the Brahma Sutras and the Bhagavat Gita: Advaita, Visistaadvaita and Dvaita. The advaita system of Shankara affirmed the oneness of the human soul with the divine (*Jeevo Brahmaiva na parah*) and proposed the path of wisdom, *jnana marga*, for spiritual liberation. The visistaadvaita system of Ramanuja held that creation together with human souls are not identical with God but part of God or the body of God; he proposed the path of surrender, *bhakti marga*. The dvaita system of Madhva held that creation and human souls are essentially different from God and proposed the path of devotion or surrender and action, *bhakti marga* and *karma marga*. The common element of these three systems is that they believe that there is only one God, one eternal reality. All these systems identify themselves as Hinduism. These three systems still hold today their diverging views.

The Biblical Tradition

Christianity comes from the Biblical tradition. We can also see a continuous growth in divine-human relationship in the Biblical tradition. In the Hebrew tradition the initial relationship with the sacred was Totemism in which a particular clan associates with a particular animal (or plant), which becomes sacred and cannot be killed. Later it developed into polytheism in which there was the worship of many gods. Albert. C. Knudson writes: 'the sole godhead of Yahweh was a truth that was only gradually attained... It was to Moses that the establishment of Yahweh worship was due. Previous to his time the Israelites seem to have been polytheists.'[94] Y. Kaufmann says, 'the Israelites were heirs to a religious tradition which can only have been polytheistic'. It is unlikely that there was a direct jump from polytheism to monotheism—they needed to pass through henotheism in which one God is presented as supreme over the other gods. H. Keith Beebe says, 'it seems clear enough... that Moses was not a monotheist, yet to call him a polytheist seems inaccurate too. We can conclude that Moses stood somewhere between Totemism and monotheism. A term to describe this position is henotheism'.[95]

Monotheism developed from henotheism—in monotheism the Hebrew prophets affirmed the existence of only one God. Other gods were nothing but dust on the scales. In this level, God is the creator and human beings are creatures of God and there is a gulf between God and human beings. No one can see God and live. God reveals his will through the Commandments. The Torah becomes the will of God.

Although the Hebrew prophets foresaw a further revelation, a New Covenant, in which God would write the Law in the hearts of the people,[96] it was with Jesus Christ that Hebrew monotheism grew into a higher level of divine-human relationship.

At the moment of his baptism, Jesus transcended the prophetic monotheistic[97] experience of God and realized himself as the Son of God. Not a creature of God but the Son of God, the incarnation of God. The Hebrew tradition did not have words to describe this experience. It did not have any memory of that experience. Hebrew prophets used words like 'New Covenant', 'New Heart', a 'Heart of flesh', 'New Jerusalem' and so on. This experience of Jesus was completely new to the Jewish tradition. It was the reason why Jewish religious leaders thought that Jesus was blaspheming. In this experience Jesus inaugurated the New Covenant.

He did not remain at this stage however but went further and realized that God and he were one, 'the Father and I are one'[98]. This statement also shocked the Jewish spiritual leaders. That was the last stage of his ascending journey. This experience is similar to that of the Upanishad statement *ayatman brahma (atman is brahman)*. But Jesus did not remain on this level either; he descended back to his human level since he had his physical body and had to live in the world of time and space in human relationships.

If we use the Vedantic categories we can say that Jesus, in his experience, moved from dvaita[99] to visistaadvaita and from there to advaita. Dvaita is the experience of being essentially different from God. Visistaadvaita is the experience of being the Son of God and advaita is the experience of being one with God. But in Jesus these three experiences were not exclusive of each other, they were integrated. He is three in one: Shankara, Ramanuja and Madhva. It is the integration of these three experiences that makes Jesus' experience of God original. He is Shankara in as much as he accepts the oneness of his human consciousness with God (the Father and I are one)[100]. He is Ramanuja in as much as he accepts that he is the Son of God or manifestation of God (I am in the Father and the Father is in me)[101]. He is Madhva in as much as he accepts that there is certain functional distance between God and himself as human, (my Father is greater than me)[102]. Jesus is one with God, he is the Son of God and he is also a human being. He is fully human and fully divine. We cannot place Jesus in any one of these systems exclusively. We need to coin a new word. His experience can be described as Integral Dynamic Monotheism (cf. chapter 13). Jesus shares with all humans his oneness with God: 'as Thou, Father, are in me and I in You, may they also be in us.'[103]

The contribution of Jesus to his spiritual tradition was that he elevated the love of God and expanded the love of neighbour. He elevated the love of God from creator-creature relationship to 'God and I are one'. We can say that he elevated it from dualistic love to non-dualistic love. That was a revolution in his spiritual tradition. In this way he brought his spiritual tradition close to the Vedic tradition.

Revelation is not Static but Historical
We can see how in both traditions there has been a unique but comparable evolution of human consciousness from the lower to the higher level–thanks to the marvellous work of divine grace. In the Vedic tradition we move from nature-worship to non-dualism and in the biblical tradition we move from polytheism to Christian non-dualism.

Jesus evolves from dualism (my Father is greater than me) to qualified non-dualism (I am in the Father and the Father is in me) and from qualified non-dualism to non-dualism (the Father and I are one).

It means that the way we experience God and understand truth depends on which level we stand. Revelation is not something static but dynamic. As we grow in our spiritual life our understanding of God and scripture also grows. In both traditions human consciousness reached its highest level even though their approaches were different. In the Vedic tradition the journey passed through intellectual enquiry and interior growth to find one's true self or proper relationship with God–whereas in the Biblical tradition the journey passed through the search for the will of God in a personal relationship with God. The end result is similar but each is unique.

In our relationship with God there is an ascending journey and there is also a descending journey. We need to ascend from creator-creature relationship (dualism) to father/mother-son/daughter relationship (qualified non-dualism) and from there to the experience of oneness with God (non-dualism). Then we also need to descend back to qualified non-dualism and dualism as long as we live in our physical body and live in this world of time and space.

SIX TYPES OF REVELATIONS

I would like to propose six types of revelations of God through which human beings grow in their relationship with God.

1. *The God of History*

This corresponds to the experience of God in time and space. This is the experience of God in the initial stages of human consciousness. Here the author has in mind particularly the God of Abraham, of Isaac and of Jacob. God manifested himself to Abraham, Isaac and Jacob and they responded to his call. They were the patriarchs of the Jewish tradition. Here the relationship was very much personal. There was not yet an established religion with laws and structures.

2. *The God of Transcendence*

When Moses asked God his name, first God replied 'I AM WHO I AM'. This is the revelation of the God of eternity who transcends time and space and who cannot be described by anything that is finite. The Jews were not allowed to make any image of God. Then God told Moses that he was the God of Abraham, Isaac and Jacob. This revelation was a very important one as it revealed that God has two aspects: eternal and historical. 'I AM WHO I AM' is the eternal aspect and 'the God of Abraham, Isaac and Jacob' is the God of history. The Upanishads describe the Ultimate Reality or God by saying 'not this, not this', neti, neti.

3. *Revelation as a Book as Commandments*

God gave Moses Ten Commandments in which he told the Jewish people what they should and shouldn't do. The love of God and the love of neighbour are the essence of the Torah. The Torah became the word of God. Here we have the experience of the God of authority, who demands the obedience or submission of will and intellect and absolute loyalty. There is a gulf between God and his/her creatures. The holy book becomes the voice of God. It becomes the sacred scripture. To obey the holy book is to obey God. With sacred scriptures a formal religion is established—with laws, rituals and authority.

4. *Limitations of the God of History and of Commandments*

This is not a positive revelation but a negative revelation. Though God gave commandments, not all people were faith ful to their God. Some continually broke the commandments and God sent the prophets to call them back to the Law. God told them they were stiff-necked and rebellious. If laws are not the self-understanding of the people but are imposed from outside then there is always a possibility of breaking them. In the evolution of human consciousness there comes a stage where human beings feel that God is too authoritative and they long for freedom from that authority. Human beings would like to have the freedom to think, to decide and to act responsibly. As long as God exists human beings think that they cannot be free, as God has already determined what they should think, will and act. Here we have the 'death of God' philosophy. This 'death of God' refers to the God of history and not to the God of eternity. Agnosticism, Secularism and

Atheism belong to this level. Although there is no positive 'revelation' here, this stage nevertheless purifies the revelation of the God of history and authority.

Atheism is a kind of fire that purifies the God of history. It shows the limitations of the images of God presented by religions. So we can call it as 'purifying revelation'. We should not look at it judgmentally but as something that belongs to the evolutionary process of our human consciousness. It is not the final stage. If human beings are aware of the God of eternity from the beginning of their spiritual evolution then this revelation may not be necessary. It may take the form of Apophatic theology. Since some religions tend to transform the revelation of the God of history into something absolute, this 'purifying revelation' seems to be a necessity. This revelation is a transition from the God of history to the God of eternity, from the God of authority to the God of freedom, from the God of words to the God of silence, from the truth outside to the truth within, from the way outside to the way inside.

5. *Revelation of the New Covenant or Universal mind*
God promised Jewish people that he would establish a New Covenant in the future in which he would write the Law in the hearts of all people. From the least to the greatest everyone will know the Lord and there will be no need for one person telling another how to know God. God will forgive their sins and he will not remember their sins any more.[104] In the New Covenant God does not reveal what people should and shouldn't do. God does not reveal a Book, God reveals 'who people are'. This revelation is also the revelation of the universal mind, in which a person is united with everyone and everything and whatever this person does to others he/she does to himself/herself. Jesus said, 'whatever you wish others to do to you, you do to them. This is the Law and the prophets'.[105] The entire Law is summarized into one: love

your neighbour as yourself.[106] In the universal mind a person does not strictly need a religion, a scripture and an authority. The reason being that for this person there are no others except God. He or she is all. This person has authority even over sacred scriptures. Jesus said, 'it is written in your Law but I say unto you'.[107] He was greater than scripture. In this level God will be experienced as indwelling presence, Emmanuel, as freedom and silence. Human beings will live from this inner wisdom and light and declare 'I am the way, the truth and the life'.[108]

To say 'I am the way, the truth and the life' is a statement of greatness and also of humility. It is a statement of greatness because a person is completely free from the past and lives in the eternal present–this person does not follow anyone from the past but lives an original and creative life. This is also a statement of humility because this person does not become a way for others or to the future. He invites everyone to live the same way of life. He invites everyone to live in the eternal present. Jesus told Nicodemus: 'the wind blows where it pleases but you do not know from where it comes nor where it goes. So it is with everyone who is born of the spirit.'[109] It is freedom from the past and freedom from the future. It is to manifest the eternity of God here and now. It is the life of the kingdom of God. It is Sanathana dharma, the eternal religion. It is to be in the realm of originality and creativity in which no one enters the tracks left by others and no one leaves tracks for others to follow. Everyone lives an original and creative life. Not to enter the tracks left by others is greatness and not to leave tracks for others is humility. 'No one tells the other to know God because everyone knows God'.[110] This is the experience of the new covenant or universal mind.

This new covenant is not really new–it is the 'eternal covenant' written in the hearts of human beings when they are born. God does not write anything *new* but allows us to realize 'who we are' from all eternity. This is what happened to Jesus at the moment of his baptism. God did not give him any commandments–even the two great commandments–but revealed who Jesus was: 'you are my beloved son'.[111] This is the revelation of the eternal Word–the source of all sacred books that no sacred book can exhaust. With this God says everything. In the New Testament God speaks only twice: at Jesus' baptism and at his transfiguration. On both occasions he says the same thing: 'you are my beloved Son' and 'he is my beloved Son'.[112] It is the revelation of the universal mind. At which God falls silent because there is nothing more to say. This is writing the law in the hearts of the people or revealing the universal mind.

To discover the universal mind is to re-enter the Garden of Eden. It is to discover one's original wholeness and fullness. It is to find the hidden treasure,[113] to find the pearl of great value.[114] It is to live in the universal presence of God. It is to walk with God in the cool of the evening. It is to go beyond fear of hell and greediness for heaven. It is to go beyond reward and punishment. The sacred books and religions came after the fall of humanity. They were not there in the beginning. A person who enters into the universal mind does not initiate a new religion, nor does he/she reveal a new book or become an authority for others. His/her primary mission will be to invite everyone to discover the universal mind and live from there. He/she is only a messenger who brings the invitation from God to humanity to enter into this new life. If he/she gives some precepts or initiates an organization they are only meant to do what he/she did: to invite people into this new life and facilitate their growth, and nothing more. Jesus invited humanity to this new life with one word: repent. It is an invitation to enter into the universal mind, to re-enter into the Garden of Eden.

6. Revelation that Human Consciousness is one with the Divine Consciousness

The revelation that human beings share in the divine nature. At this level a person declares, 'God and I are one', 'I am Brahman'. Jesus said, 'the Father and I are one'. In Jesus we can all say that God and I are one. This is the last stage in the ascending journey of our human consciousness. These statements need to be understood very carefully because there is always a danger of misinterpreting them–thinking that a human being is God. The 'I' which says that 'God and I are one' is not an 'individual I' or a 'collective I' or a 'universal I' but a 'divine I'. It is God who says I am Brahman, I am God.

Our human consciousness is like a bridge between the divine and our lower nature, body and mind. It is like a reflection of the divine in the mirror of the body and mind. When this reflection identifies with the body and mind it feels like a creature but when it looks into its source, the divine, it says 'God and I are one'. Our human consciousness is God's breath[115] into our earthen vessel. It is God's seed[116] in us having the potential to grow into the divine.

In the fifth revelation human beings discover universal consciousness. In the sixth revelation universal consciousness enters or grows into divine consciousness. When they enter into the divine, the whole of humanity and the whole of creation enter into God. It is the experience of the whole of humanity and the whole of creation merging into God. The reflection realizes its source. It is as if the whole of creation has dissolved into God, it is as if it is the end of the world. It moves to the state before God manifested creation. In this experience a person discovers the redemption of the whole of humanity and the whole of creation in the unconditional love of God. A person discovers the good news for the whole of humanity and the whole of creation. It is not the experience of a single individual even though the journey is happening in a particular physical individual. Jesus said, 'no one has ascended into heaven except the Son of Man who descended from heaven.'[117] Jesus is the Son of Man, representing the whole of creation. In as much as he has descended from God, he is the manifestation of God. He also ascended into heaven and in him the whole of creation has returned to God. He is the saviour of the whole of humanity and creation. This experience is like climbing onto the roof of a house: one cannot live there but has to descend again and integrate the lower levels–which are our human aspects–so that divinity and humanity can be united and integrated. A person who realizes this truth becomes very humble as he/she knows that every human being has the same potential even though they may not know it. This person invites everyone to discover this truth and tries to facilitate that realization. This person may withdraw from the world or involve with the world according to the will of God that he/she feels within.

But human beings are not only rooted in the divine in their ultimate level, they are also human as long as they live in the world of time and space and in human relationships. Ascending humanity is elevated to divinity because descending divinity incarnates into humanity. It is divinized humanity. This is why the Greek Fathers spoke of divinization. Jesus described this with a simple parable: 'the Kingdom of God is like a woman who took yeast and put in three measure of meal or flour until it was leavened'.[118] The flour is our humanity and yeast is our divinity. Our humanity is divinized. Christians believe that Christ is fully divine and fully human. The consciousness of Jesus is like a bridge between divinity and humanity. On one side he is divine and on the other he is human. In him divinity and humanity are integrated. All humans are called to become one with Christ and live his experience.

The first three revelations belong to the God of history and the last two belong to the God of eternity. The fourth one is a transition from the God of history to the God of eternity. We can say that Jesus, at the moment of his baptism, moved from the God of history to the God of eternity, from the God of authority to the God of freedom, from the First Covenant to the New Covenant. Jesus declared: 'before Abraham was I am'.[119] He transcended the God of Abraham (history) and experienced unity with the God of 'I am who I am' (eternity). The Mundaka Upanishad speaks of two types of wisdom: Para Vidhya and Apara Vidhya, higher wisdom and lower wisdom. Lower wisdom belongs to the God of history and higher wisdom belongs to the God of eternity. We begin with the God of history and then we need to move into the God of eternity. These two are not exclusive. The God of eternity includes the God of history. We can say that the God of history is the womb of God in which God nourishes humanity before he/she gives birth to them into the God of eternity.

The Fullness of Revelation

The purpose of every revelation is to tell us who we are and how we have to live our lives in the temporal and spatial world. The fullness of revelation reveals that we are ultimately grounded in God. This is the radical love of God. It affirms divinity as our foundation and humanity as its manifestation. The fullness of revelation also reveals that we, as manifestations of God, need to live in loving relationships. Human life is relationship and in relationships we experience God. We need to see every human being as the manifestation of God and every creature as the manifestation of God and love them as such. We need to show special love and care to those who most need it. 'Whatever you do to the least of my brothers and sisters that you do unto me,'[120] is the expression of the fullness of revelation regarding the love of neighbour. It is the radical love of neighbour.

Traditional Judaism[121] and Islam[122] and Christianity focus very much on the revelation of the Book, the Torah and the Holy Koran. The entire focus is on the literal interpretations of the Holy Books. Human beings cannot go beyond the Book.

According to these three prophetic religions human beings are primarily creatures of God. There is a gulf between God and human beings. Even after death human beings will be separate from God even if they exist in God's presence. There is no emptying of oneself into the divine. These religions deny human beings not only their divine son-ship and daughter-ship but also their radical experience of God. Human beings are just creatures of God. The emphasis is on our humanness.

The theory of creation out of nothing forbids the evolution of human consciousness into higher levels. Though this theory appears to be a satisfying theory it is not a very liberating theory since it keeps people eternally separate from God. It is a somewhat oppressive theory. In Christianity an exception is made of Jesus Christ: he is a human being, the Son of God and one with God. However, only Jesus Christ has this possibility. He is seen as essentially different from the rest of human beings. And yet St. Paul insists that by grace we are 'in Christ' and St. Peter tells us that we 'share in the divine nature'.[123]

The advaitic system of Hinduism holds that the human soul is ultimately one with the divine (Jeevo Brahmaiva Na parah). Only God is eternal (Brahma sathyam) and creation is unreal or an illusion (Jagat

Mithya). The focus is entirely on our divinity—our humanity melts into the ocean of the divine. It tends to neglect our humanity. The visistadvaitic system of Hinduism holds that human beings are part of God, manifestations of God. God is qualified by human souls and creation. It rescues a little bit of our humanness. Human beings can be sons and daughters of God and can have a personal relationship with God. But they are not equal with the divine. There is a subtle essential difference between God and human souls. We are no longer melted into the ocean of the divine but are as icebergs (made of water) on the ocean (of water). But it denies our divinity and humanness. The dvaitic system of Madhva holds that human beings are essentially different from God. They are essentially and primarily creatures of God. Human consciousness is rather like solid earth, different but bordering on the divine ocean. There is a gulf between God and human beings—this strengthens their distance and relationship. But it rather denies our possibility of realizing our divine son-ship and daughter-ship and denies too our sharing in the divine nature. (It should be mentioned that the Hindu theological systems do not accept the theory of creation out of nothing.)

Fully Human-Fully divine

Each system, by emphasizing one aspect, neglects the other aspects. Only in the integration of these three aspects can human beings experience the fullness of revelation. It is my opinion that in Jesus Christ this integration has taken place and he opened this possibility to everyone. This is the good news of Jesus to humanity.

Jesus said: 'I am the light of the world'[124] and 'you are the light of the world'.[125] These two statements are the summary of Jesus' good news. They are the two sides of the same coin (one without the other is only half-truth). He invited humanity to discover this truth or to grow into this truth with the statement 'the kingdom of God is at hand, repent'.[126] The entire message of Jesus is contained in this one word 'repent'. It is an invitation to people to the great banquet of the kingdom of God. The banquet is ready, please come and eat. It is an invitation to eat at the divine table. It is the banquet where human nature is divinized and divine becomes human. It is the banquet where God offers himself/herself as the food and drink of immortality to human beings–and human beings offer themselves to God as food and drink to be transformed into immortality. God eats us and we eat God. God drinks us and we drink God. It is the banquet of spiritual transformation, spiritual alchemy. We need to elevate our humanity towards divinity and bring down divinity towards our humanity. Our divine son-ship and daughter-ship is the bridge between our human pole and divine pole. It is the centre that holds these two together.

Realizing unity with our divine foundation does not make us proud, it makes us humble. Many people misunderstand the statement 'God and I are one'. They think it is an arrogant and blasphemous statement. On the face it appears like that. In fact it is the most humble statement anyone can make. It does not mean a human being becomes God. No human being can become God. If every human being becomes God then there will be billions of Gods in the world. There are no gods but God. It only means to realize that God alone is and we all come from God and return to God. It may be wise to say, 'my true self is God' or 'my foundation is God' rather than saying 'God and I are one' or 'I am God'.

Many people think that if we say 'we are the creatures of God' we are very humble. In fact we are not humble but very proud–it is a blasphemy. We are creating a reality separate from God. It is a sin because we have no separate existence apart from God. A Sufi master said: 'my own existence is my greatest sin'.[127] It signifies having a separate existence apart from God. Jesus realized that he was one with God and then he washed the feet of his disciples. We can see the humility of a person who realized his unity with God. This is the uniqueness of Jesus. The deeper a person grows into God the more humble a person becomes. The virtue of humility is the sign of our spiritual maturity. It is possible that later corruption can enter and the followers of that person can manipulate this experience for their own power and self-glorification. When Jesus said 'the Father and I are one' the Jewish religious authorities misunderstood him. They thought he was blaspheming. In fact he was making a very humble statement.

In Christianity God spoke his final 'Word' through his Son.[128] This final Word is the revelation of human consciousness being in the ultimate level one with divine consciousness. This revelation was not present in the Jewish tradition. The Jewish tradition foresaw the universal mind (the New Covenant) but not the oneness of human consciousness with divine consciousness.

This revelation was already there in the Vedic tradition five hundred years before Jesus. The Upanishad sages had already realized this truth through their spiritual enquiry propelled by the grace of God. The originality of the revelation of Christ is the marriage of the radical love of God with the radical love of neighbour. It is the marriage of wisdom and action in love. Love is wisdom manifesting in action.

Jesus said that the queen of Sheba came to listen to the Wisdom of Solomon but someone greater than Solomon is here. The people of Nineveh listened to the voice of Prophet Jonah but someone greater than prophet Jonah is here. Solomon was considered to be wise but his wisdom was dualistic wisdom. With all his wisdom Solomon could never have said: 'the Father (God) and I are one'. Jesus said it. A prophet invites people to the love of neighbour, to the love of the poor, the orphans and widows. Jonah represented this love of neighbour. But this love was dualistic love. A neighbour is someone other than us. Jesus went beyond this dualistic love. His love was non-dualistic love: 'whatever you do to the least of my brothers and sisters that you do unto me'.

Non-dualistic Wisdom and Non-dualistic Action

In Jesus non-dualistic wisdom and non-dualistic action come together in love. It was the marriage of wisdom and action. This is the fullness of truth that Jesus came to reveal, the fullness of revelation to which he bore witness. This is the kingdom of God. He invited his listeners to realize this truth.

The religious authorities of his time were not ready for this truth, particularly the unity of human consciousness and divine consciousness in one person. They considered it blasphemous and Jesus had to be crucified. The crucifixion of Jesus was the consequence of Jesus standing by his spiritual realization and the refusal of Jewish spiritual authorities to accept his message and to grow in divine-human and human-human relationships. Jesus had to stand by his spiritual realization for the spiritual evolution of human consciousness even though he knew that it would cost his life. He accepted his death for the spiritual liberation of humanity. He had to lay down his life on the cross in order to open the door for the spiritual evolution of humanity. Jesus died for spiritual growth, for unity, for liberation, particularly spiritual liberation. Even today whenever we refuse to grow in divine-human relationship and human-human relationships we are crucifying Jesus Christ.

His primary mission was not to reform his religion, not to give a new Book (he did not write a thing!), not to start a new religion, but to inaugurate the new covenant, to inaugurate a new human consciousness, to inaugurate the universal mind, which can claim like him, 'I am the way, the truth and the life'. His mission was to invite humanity to this new life.

His message was a kind of spiritual revolution and also the fulfilment of the aspirations of his spiritual tradition. He tried to transform his religion to be a matrix for this new life. Since his religious authorities did not cooperate with his message Jesus had to form a group of close disciples as a nest to facilitate the birth of this new covenant, of new human consciousness, of universal mind. He gave them the keys of wisdom that open the door to the kingdom of God, the God of eternity. St. Paul said, 'if anyone is in Christ he or she is a new creation'.

The Challenge of the Vedic Tradition and the Vision of Christ

The Upanishad tradition emphasizes our divine pole whereas the prophetic tradition emphasizes our human pole, our essential difference from God. In Jesus Christ a marriage took place between our divinity and our humanity. He is one hundred per cent divine and one hundred per cent human. He not only affirms divinity as the ground of our existence but also our functional difference from God. He opened this possibility to every human being. Christianity, with all its good intentions, limited this possibility only to Christ and closed the door (which

Jesus had opened to everyone) to the Christians. One cannot find fault with it. In a tradition where the transcendence of God was emphasized it would have been difficult or impossible for Jesus' disciples to imagine that they too could claim to share the experience Jesus had.

To accept the possibility of that experience for one person (Jesus) was a kind of progress. Unfortunately, though understandably, that comprehension created a kind of spiritual apartheid between Christ and Christians and gave institutional power and authority to those who represent Christ. Institutional power and authority have their purpose and value (in fact they are in the plan of God), as long as they are at the service of spiritual authority and power. They are like the institution of Sabbath, which is meant to be at the service of human beings and not human beings at the service of Institution. Jesus told his listeners to obey the authority of those who sit on the seat of Moses. The power and the authority which Jesus gave to his disciples were spiritually liberating. 'Truth will make you free,' Jesus declared.

Christianity is caught up between two positions: one vision for Christians and another for Christ. When it comes to human beings it maintains the view of the prophetic tradition that human beings are creatures of God; when it comes to Christ it maintains the position of the Upanishad tradition that he is one with God. Whilst the Vedic tradition (advaitic) gives to every human being the possibility to realize one's divinity, Christianity limits it only to Jesus Christ.

This is the shortcoming of Christianity. The Upanishad tradition challenges Christianity to open the experience of the radical love of God which Jesus experienced to every Christian, not to limit it to Jesus Christ alone. Unless Christianity opens this possibility it may be recognized in India for its social services and charitable works but it cannot appeal to the deepest spiritual aspirations of the Hindu heart and mind.

In the same manner the challenge of Christ's message to the Vedic tradition would be to translate its radical love of God into radical love of neighbour. It is to translate its wisdom into socially transformative action.

A Marginal Difference and Genuine Dialogue

The difference between the Vedic vision and the vision of Jesus Christ is very marginal. These two visions are similar regarding the radical love of God. They both emphasize the need to discover God as our ultimate ground, our oneness with God. They both speak of universal consciousness that lives for the welfare of the whole world. They are also similar regarding the need for human will to become the vehicle of divine will. Jesus said, 'I have not come to do my will but the will of him who sent me' and 'Father, if it is possible take away this cup from me, but not my will, let thy will be done'.[129] Arjuna initially did not want to fight or act but then finally he says to Krishna, 'yes, I will do thy will' (Gita.18.73). They are also similar in as much as they both insist on the necessity of action. Life should manifest in action. They both speak of love as wisdom manifesting in action. Jesus said, 'my father is working and so I am also working'. Krishna tells Arjuna to follow his action of non-action. Arjuna has to act or fight. Jesus would not deny the process of karma and reincarnation but only his reaction to it would be different from the Vedic tradition and from the Gita.

It is the strong emphasis on the love of neighbour, the marginalized in society and socially transformative action that distinguishes the vision of Jesus from the vision of Vedic sages and the Bhagavat Gita. It also changes the way one experiences God. Jesus presents a God who is unconditional love. He does not sit above in the heavens and wait for people to find him but comes down to this world in search of lost humanity as a shepherd goes in search of his lost sheep. He does not come into the world in order to remove un-righteousness (a-dharma) and to establish righteousness (dharma) but to call both the righteous and the unrighteous into the kingdom of God which is beyond moral righteousness and moral un-righteousness. He said, 'unless your righteousness transcends that of the scribes and the Pharisees (morally righteous people), you cannot enter into the kingdom of heaven'. He admonished the scribes and the Pharisees saying that the sinners, the tax collectors and the prostitutes are entering the kingdom before them.[130]

For Jesus spiritual life is not a battle between good people and bad people. It is not about good destroying bad—it is discovering the absolute good which transcends both relative good and relative bad. It is seeing the limitations of relative good and seeing the possibilities for relative bad. It is seeing both good and bad as the children of God. The purpose of incarnation is not to deliver the righteous and destroy the unrighteous and establish righteousness—but to take human consciousness beyond the battlefield between the righteous and the unrighteous into the unconditional love of God and peace. It is to change swords into ploughshares and spears into sickles.

Hinduism presents mukthi or liberation as freedom from birth and death. Being born in this world is seen as something negative, a consequence of one's previous actions. So Hindus strive to be free from birth and death. For Jesus salvation is not freedom from physical birth and death. To be born in this world is not something negative.

Every birth is a unique manifestation of God. Human beings are destined to be vehicles of the divine and unfold divine attributes of love and compassion in human relationships.

For Jesus realizing our oneness with God is not the end of our purpose in life–it is just the beginning. In one sense our purpose ends but God's purpose begins. Salvation is right relationship with God and with one another. It is freedom from the movement of ego, from ignorance and from desires against human dignity. The goal is not be free from birth and death but to be continuous manifestations of God.

The Gita also presents the need to be free from ego, from desire, from ignorance and exhorts right relationship between God and human soul. It presents the relationship between Krishna and Arjuna as an ideal relationship. Krishna acts in and through Arjuna and they exist eternally. Jesus Christ is both God and human, Krishna and Arjuna. In one level he is God and in another level he is human. His humanity is at the service of the divine.

Jesus presents God as being close to the poor, the sinners and the broken hearted. God is at the service of humanity. God wishes to establish a just and equal society based on the values of the kingdom of God. God is the God of social justice.

Jesus needed to die a violent death on the cross like a criminal as he tried to transform society according to the vision of the radical love of God and radical love of neighbour. Today many Hindu movements are also involved in charitable works and socially transformative action. Hence the difference between Vedic vision and the vision of Christ is very marginal. It seems to me that the differences are more theoretical than actual or practical. A genuine and sincere dialogue can bring these two religions together easily. If that happens, three to four billion people in the world will be united. What an exciting thing to hope for? To facilitate this dialogue Christianity needs to grow into the inclusive vision of Christ and recognize the grace of God manifested in the Vedic tradition.

SATHYAM–TRUTH

In Chandogya Upanishad[131] there is an interesting analysis of the word for truth. The word for truth is sathyam, comprising the elements sat-ti-yam. *'Sat'* means that which exists by itself—it is eternal, infinite. *'Ti'* means that whose existence depends on something else. It is temporal, non-eternal and finite. *'Yam'* means that which holds or binds these two, sat and ti, so it becomes sathyam. So truth is the union of the infinite and the finite, God and creation. But the infinite and finite are always united. They can never be separated. The finite can never exist without the support of the infinite, like a tree cannot exist without the support of the earth. It is our ignorance that makes us see the infinite and finite as separate. It builds an artificial wall between them. When human beings break free from ignorance then they see the already existing unity between these two. The finite is seen as the manifestation of God, as the body and blood of God. So if, by fullness of revelation or truth, we mean the integration of humanity with divinity, the finite with the infinite, the temporal with the eternal then Christians can say that Jesus Christ is the fullness of truth, sathyam. In him the divinity and humanity, the infinite and the finite, the eternal and the temporal are united.

The description of Truth according to Chandogya Upanishad is very beautiful but it sounds very static. Truth is not only unity of the infinite with the finite—it is also dynamic. It is manifesting in action, in relationships. In General the Upanishads propose the path of wisdom to self-realization in opposition to the path of action. The Isa Upanishad and the Bhagavat Gita add dynamism to this static description of Truth. The Isa Upanishad insists on the importance of wisdom manifesting in action. In the Bhagavat Gita Krishna advises Arjuna that action must not be renounced but it should be done without expecting any reward. It should come from wisdom. The essence of the Bhagavat Gita is the marriage of wisdom and action in Love. To this dynamism of truth Jesus adds the aspect of love of neighbour, the marginalized and social transformation. For Jesus truth is unity manifesting in human relationships because life is relationships. It is the integration of the radical love of God with the radical love of neighbour. It is transforming our human actions into divine actions. This love of neighbour is not an obligation, not a burden, it is not result-oriented, nor to purify oneself, nor to acquire merit—rather it is a spontaneous expression that comes from the realization that we are all in God. It comes from inner freedom. It is meant to manifest the divine attributes in loving human relationships.

The love of neighbour does not mean just helping the poor and so on. Foremost it is seeing everyone as the manifestations of God and relating with them as such—this leads to helping those people who are in need physically, economically, socially, intellectually, politically, psychologically and spiritually. Ultimately it signifies helping people to find the kingdom of God, to experience the kingdom of God. It also means loving oneself. It is to love God as oneself and love the neighbour as oneself because we are all one in God. Jesus loved God as himself and he loved every human being and creation as himself. In the Isa Upanishad we read, 'a sage does not hurt himself by hurting others' because, for a sage, others do not exist. He or she is one with everyone.

Eucharist and the Truth

Jesus revealed the essence of his truth through the celebration of the Eucharist. The Eucharist is the dynamic expression of the Truth. It is the expression of the kingdom of God. It is the essence of the radical love of God and the radical love of neighbour. It is the realization of the unity of the finite with the infinite. It is the transformation of the finite into infinite. The bread and wine represent the whole of creation and humanity. By elevating them Jesus transformed them into divine, into body and blood of God, into manifestations of God. In fact it is not really transforming them but seeing them already as manifestations of God because they are already the manifestation of God. It is not so much elevating the bread and the wine but it is elevating one's own consciousness. It is our ignorance that throws a veil over that truth. Jesus was free from ignorance so he was able to see the reality of creation as the manifestation of God. He realized himself as the body and blood of God. There are three ways we can look at the creation: dualistic, qualified non-dualistic and non-dualistic. From the dualistic point of view creation is essentially different from God. From the qualified non-dualistic point of view creation is the manifestation of God. It is the body and blood of God. There is a subtle difference between God and creation; they are not one in being. From the non-dualistic point of view creation is one in being with God but different in manifestation.

The elevation of the bread and wine is elevating our human consciousness from the dualistic experience to the qualified non-dualistic experience and from there to the non-dualistic experience so that we discover that we are one with God at the source and we are also manifestations of God. It is ascending from dualistic experience of God into qualified non-dualistic experience of God and from there into non-dualistic experience of God. This is the experience of the radical love of God. This is our ascending journey.

Then he gave the bread and wine to his disciples and said: this is my body, take and eat. This is my blood, take and drink. This is the radical love of neighbour. This is his descending aspect. He had to come down from non-dualistic experience to the qualified non-dualistic experience and from there to dualism. He had to come back to the dualistic experience as long as he lived in the physical body and lived in the world of time and space. He had to become food to his brothers and sisters. It is to give and receive in loving relationships. The Eucharist reveals that life is a celebration. It is a ritual, a liturgy, a sacrament. Jesus did not celebrate the Eucharist only at the last supper but throughout his life–from his baptismal experience onwards, his life was a continuous Eucharistic celebration, a liturgy, a ritual, a celebration and a sacrament. The last supper was only an audiovisual presentation of his life, his experience and his essential message before his departure from this world so that his disciples would not forget it. To eat the body and to drink the blood of Jesus is to enter into the consciousness of Jesus. It is to turn our life also into a continuous Eucharistic celebration. We become what we eat.

Then Jesus said: do this in memory of me[132]. We need to do what Jesus did. We need to celebrate this Eucharist. We need to elevate our human pole towards the divine pole. That is to ascend from dualism to non-dualism. This is our radical love of God. Then we need to descend from non-dualism to dualism. This is our radical love of neighbour. We need to become body and blood to our brothers and sisters. Life is to give and to receive. It is the breaking of the bread. The disciples going to Emmaus recognized Jesus in the breaking of the bread. So it is in the breaking of the bread, which is giving and receiving, that we encounter Jesus, that we celebrate the Eucharist. All our actions become a Eucharistic celebration. Our entire life becomes a Eucharistic celebration. The ultimate purpose of our human existence is to transform our actions into actions of God. It is to transform our life into the life of God. This is the real Eucharistic celebration. This is the coming of the kingdom of God. Jesus said, 'the works which I do are not my own but the Father who dwells in me does his works'.

In Jesus, the kingdom of God was manifesting in its fullness. Every time when we say 'thy kingdom come', we are praying for the coming of the kingdom of God in our lives. Jesus said, 'first of all seek you the kingdom of God and its righteousness and all things will be given unto you'. The primary purpose of our human existence is to seek the will of God and surrender ourselves to God and allow God to live and work in us. Then it is the responsibility of God to provide all our needs.

Conclusion

Truth is like a circle. Our journey is like a dot that begins at the centre of the circle and grows vertically and horizontally until it reaches the circumference. Growing vertically is growing into the love of God and growing horizontally is growing towards the love of neighbour.

It becomes a cross. Some people may be more attracted vertically and some may be attracted more horizontally. Some may stop on the way and may not fill the circle. As human beings evolve there will be always some imbalances. The good news is that no one is outside this circle and no truth is outside this circle. In the case of Jesus this journey was complete—it reached its end, both vertically and horizontally.

Jesus came into the world to reveal and bear witness to the truth, to the kingdom of God, to the good news, to the unconditional love of God, to the radical love of God and the radical love of neighbour.

No truth can go beyond that and no revelation can go beyond that. This truth cannot be crammed into any belief structure or moral structure or into any philosophical system, theological system or political system. At the same time this truth does not exclude any person, any system of truth or any religion or any spiritual practice. Any path or practice that helps human beings grow into love of God and love of neighbour is accepted. It sees conditioned truth in every system. It embraces all concepts of truth and transcends all of them. All systems can act only as a platform from which human beings need to grow. Every system has some truth in it. A system is like a room with walls and a roof. There is space within these walls in which people can live. That space is a truth but it is a conditioned truth. If we make conditioned truth absolute then it becomes exclusive. The kingdom of God is all inclusive. It is alive and dynamic. It embodies in a person not in a system. It does not have a boundary.

Jesus said that 'the foxes have their holes and the birds have their nests but the son of man has nowhere to lie down and rest'.[133] He was living in the infinite truth, in *sanathana dharma*. Jesus also said that 'the kingdom of God is like a mustard seed. It is the smallest of all seeds but when it grows it becomes so big that the birds of the air will come and make their nests in it'.[134] The kingdom of God is so big that it embraces all the conditioned truths (nests) that people construct–but transcends them. The conditioned truths are like nests which act as a preparatory ground to move into the freedom of the kingdom of God. If the conditioned truths are made absolute then they become cages in which people imprison themselves. Therefore we can say that in Jesus Christ we have the fullness of truth and the fullness of revelation.[135] He was the personification of the kingdom of God, the radical love of God and the radical love of neighbour. These two are the criteria to evaluate every truth. Jesus invited his listeners to grow into this fullness of truth. He entrusted his disciples with the mission to realize this truth, to proclaim this truth and to bear witness to it.

16.
TRUTH

Sathya Prema—which signifies truth manifesting in love—was a great sage. She taught that they are five aspects to the Truth: Sat[136], Sathyam[137], Sathya Vidhya[138], Sathya Jnana[139] and Sathya Prema[140].

Sathyanvesi—which means seeker of Truth—came to Sathya Prema at the age of twelve and lived with her for twelve years as her spiritual student. She served her mistress with love and dedication. She studied all the spiritual sciences. At the end of her stay, Sathya Prema said to Sathyanvesi: 'my daughter, before you depart, if you have any questions, you may ask me.' Sathyanvesi asked her teacher, 'Mother, I have studied so many subjects, but I have not yet understood the essence of all this knowledge. Can you tell me in few words what truth is?'

Sathya Prema was very pleased with Sathyanvesi's question. She replied: 'My daughter, there are five aspects to the Truth.

The first aspect is Sat: Sat is that which exists by itself. Its existence does not depend on anything else. There is only one Sat or only one God. It is Sat or Truth before the manifestation of creation. If you negate everything that is finite, asat, what remains is Sat or Truth. So, at the first level Truth is Sat or God.

The second aspect is Sathyam: it is Sat or God united with creation. Sat is infinite and ti is finite. Ti cannot exist by itself. Its existence completely depends on Sat. Yam is the union of these two. Hence Sathyam is the union of God and creation. It is God after the creation has come into being. Sat is God without the creation–Sathyam is God with the creation.

The third aspect is Sathya Vidhya: it is the knowledge about Sat and creation. It is the construction of the intellectual systems regarding the nature of God, nature of creation and the relationship between God and creation. This is also present in all the sacred scriptures. This is what you have learned in these twelve years.

The fourth aspect is Sathya Jnana: it is the direct experience of Sat in which a person realizes oneness with Sat. In this experience all the desires of the human heart are fulfilled. One finds the essence of one's learning and experience. Intellectual knowledge becomes experiential knowledge. Knowledge becomes wisdom. The seeker and the sought become one.

The fifth aspect is Sathya Prema: it is Sathya Jnana, wisdom manifesting in loving relationships. It is the loving (Prema) relationship between finite beings rooted in the unity of God and creation. Whatever a person does, he or she does to himself or herself. It is the radical love of God and the radical love of neighbour. It is non-dualistic wisdom manifesting in non-dualistic action.

My daughter, you need to grow from Sathya Vidhya to Sathya Jnana, from Sathya Jnana to Sathya Prema–Sathya Vidhya finds its fulfilment in Sathya Jnana and Sathya Jnana finds its fulfilment in Sathyaprema. Sathyam is God with creation. When creation is no longer there then there is no Sathyam but only Sat. Ultimately what remains is Sat and we are one with that Sat, thus the expression, Sathyanvesi, *tat vam asi*. you are that[141]'.

Sathyanvesi thanked her teacher profoundly, received her blessings and went home fully satisfied.

Endnotes

1	Jer.31.31-34.	29	Jn.14.6.
2	Mk.1.11.	30	Mt.23.13.
3	Mt.3.17	31	Lk.9.51-56.
4	Mk.1.14.-15.	32	Jn.4.19-24.
5	Mt.5.20-48.	33	Jn.4.19-24
6	Jer.31.31-34.	34	Mt.3.2, Mk.1.14-15.
7	Mt.13.31.	35	Mt.6.33.
8	Jn.14.10.	36	Jn.10.30.
9	Jn.10.30	37	Mt.25.40.
10	Mt.7.13.	38	Jn.14.10.
11	Jn.5.26.	39	Mt.13.44.
12	Jn.10.10.	40	Mt.13.45.
13	Gen.3.24.	41	Mt.11.28.
14	Jer.31.31-34.	42	Mt.22.1-14
15	Jn.1.1,14.	43	Mk.1.14-15.
16	Lk.3.21-22.	44	Jn.3.3.
17	Jn.14.11.	45	Mt.18.3.
18	Jn.14.10	46	Mt.16.25.
19	Jn.10.30.	47	Jn.12.24.
20	Mt.28.18, Jn.5.19.	48	Mt.13.31-32.
21	Lk.22.42.	49	Mt.7.13.
22	Mt.18.3.	50	Jn.10.30.
23	Lk.22.42.	51	Jn.1.1.
24	Lk.15.11.32.	52	Mt.5.17.
25	Jer.31.31-34.	53	Phil. 2.6-11.
26	Mk.2.27.	54	Mt.5.8.
27	Mt.5.17.	55	Lk.11.52.
28	Jn.4.23-24.	56	Jn.14.6.

57 Mk.16.15.
58 Gita. 4.11.
59 Mk.1.14-15.
60 Mt.3.2.
61 Mk.1.11.
62 Ex.3.14.
63 Jn.16.15.
64 Mt.5.43-44.
65 Mk.1.14-15.
66 Mt.3.2.
67 Jn.3.3.
68 Mt.18.3.
69 Jn.12.24.
70 Mt.13.31-32.
71 Mt.13.45.
72 Mt.6.33.
73 Mt.13.44.
74 Gita Ch.18.
75 Brhadaranyaka Upanishad
76 Chandogya Upanishad
77 Sikhism is also a monotheistic religion but we do not speak about it.
78 Kabbala is the mystical tradition of Judaism but we do not speak about it here.
79 We do not speak about the mystical tradition of Christianity.
80 Sufism is the mystical tradition of Islam but we do not speak about it here.
81 There are total five: advaita, visistaadvaita, dvaita, bedabeda, suddadvaita.
82 There are different views on it.
83 There are different views on it.
84 Gen.2.7.
85 Jn.10.30.
86 Mt.25.40.
87 Jn.18.37.
88 Jn.10.30
89 Mt.25.40.
90 Sikhism is also a monotheistic religion and can be called a prophetic religion.
91 Prof. Max Muller used this word.

92 Rig Veda 1-164-46.
93 Atman is not individual soul. Individual soul is called Jivatman.
94 Albert C. Knudson, *The Religious Teaching of the Old Testament.*
95 Beebe, *The Old Testement*, P.160.
96 Jer.31.31.-34.
97 Prophetic monotheism believes that there is only one God and this God is the creator of the universe. Traditionally it is said that God creates the universe out of nothing. There is a gulf between God and human beings. Hindu Monotheism believes that there is only one God and this God is not the creator but manifests the creation. Jesus at the moment of his baptism transcended prophetic monotheistic experience of God and had the Hindu monotheistic experience of God. He is not a creature of god but the manifestation of God. In this sense Jesus is not a prophetic monotheist but a Hindu monotheist.
98 Jn.10.30.
99 Dvaita system believes that God and creation are eternally existing. Creation is not created by God. it is for this reason it is called dvaita. But here we use the word to mean only in the sense that human soul is essentially different from God and not as eternal
100 Jn.10.30
101 Jn.14.10-11.
102 Jn.14.28.
103 Jn.17?1
104 Jer.31.31-34.
105 Mt.7.12.
106 Deut.6.5.
107 Jn.10.34.
108 Jn.14.6.
109 Jn.3.8.
110 Jer.31..31-34.
111 Lk.3.22.
112 Mk.9.7.
113 Mt.13.44
114 Mt.13.45.
115 Gen.2.7.
116 1Jn.3.9.
117 Jn.3.13.
118 Mt.13.33
119 Jn.8.58.

120 Mt.25.40
121 We do not speak about Kabala the mystical tradition of Judaism.
122 We do not speak here, Sufism the mystical tradition of Islam.
123 2Pt.1.4.
124 Jn 8.12.
125 Mt.5.14.
126 Mt.1.14-15.
127 From memory
128 Heb.1.1.-2.
129 Mk.14.36.
130 The New Testament speaks of the Last Judgment when Jesus comes as a Judge who separates the good and the bad. The good will go to heaven and the bad to hell. This is not the teaching of Christ but the projection of the early Christian community.
131 Chandogya Upanishad 8.3.5
132 Lk.22.19
133 Mt.8.20.
134 Mt.13.31-32.
135 It is not necessary to hold the view that this revelation did not happen before him or after him.
136 Ekam Sat Vipra Bhavuti Vadanti, Rg veda.
137 Chandogya Upanishad
138 Mundaka Upanishad, Apara Vidhya
139 Mundaka Upanishad, Para Vidhya.
140 The Love taught by Christ
141 Chandogya Upanishad.

Other Books from Luc Editions

www.LucEditions.com

From the same author:

The New Annunciation
A Universal call to be virgin mothers

A superb, short book that deftly and clearly presents an overview of John's vigorous and transformative theology. A must!

From his editor, Eric Callcut:

JUDE
Transit Hall 37 North 6

JUDE
The Surface

JUDE
Adsbàn

A deep and moving science-fiction trilogy; one man's physical, personal and spiritual journey. A search for truth–exciting and transformative!

Books in French, from Eric Callcut:

Banlieue Bible
Le Sermon sur la Grande Butte

Banlieue Bible
Noël dans le Nord-Pas de Calais

More to follow!

Dépôt légal : août 2013